Welcome

We are so incredibly happy that you are here to learn wire wrapping with us!

We hope that you enjoy this book.

Contents

Introduction - 5

Getting Started

Wire Wrapping and Weaving Tools - 6
Materials: Wires, Beads - 7
Gemstones - 7
Cabochon Shapes - 10
Which Wire to Use - 10

Techniques

Double Loop Chain - 11
Beaded Loop Chain - 13
Loop Chain - 15
Lobster Clasp - 18
Wire Weaving Techniques - 21
Ear Wire - 27
Making Loops - 29

Tutorials

Classy Bead Ring - 33
Egyptian Bracelet - 39
Flawless Flame Pendant - 45
Elegant Drop Earrings - 51
Celtic Beaded Ring - 57
Beaded Bracelet - 63
Prong Settings Pendant - 69
Elegance Earrings - 75
Simple Classy Ring - 81
Grace Pendant - 87
Sun Weave Earrings - 93
Milky Way Ring - 99
Royal Beauty Pendant - 105

About

Getting Inspiration - 113
About the Author - 115

Introduction

When did it all start?
Wire wrapping is one of the most antique techniques used to create handmade jewelry. These techniques have been there forever, and there is evidence of the use of wire back to thousands of years BC, discovering wire elements in jewelry in the tombs of the pharaohs in Egypt. In the British Museum we can find jewelry of the Sumerian Dynasty dated back to 2000 BC, where they incorporated wire.
But how did they do it?
Gold has been the most popular metal in those times as it was easy to hammer it into sheets, then to be cut into strips and rolled into tubes. The long history of this art shows that it lasted for a long time because of the simplicity to create this jewelry, as there was no need to use fire or electricity or modern tools.

What is wire wrapping?
This art requires simple tools, and no soldering is needed. We will do all the work with the wire and the pliers, then we will learn how to embellish our jewelry with beads and gemstones. We will use mechanical connections instead of soldering and heat treatments. Mechanical connection is when we attach wire pieces and loops to each other by interlocking them or weaving them together.

What do I need to start?
In this book we will learn to wrap the wire around itself by multiple wire weaving techniques, and how to wrap the wire around other elements like beads and gemstone cabochons. There are many different techniques included in this book which require a basic wire and toolkit, some beads, and cabochons.
While we can find the basic toolkit on the next pages, I would like to recommend to you to stock up on some beautiful beads and gorgeous cabochons in oval, round, and teardrop shapes. In the wires section I will explain to you with more details what wires I recommend you start with, which you can find in many online shops. The tools you will need can be found in any craft or hobby store around you.

Let's start!
While the tutorials have been created with high resolution step by step pictures with the corresponding detailed and well written instructions, in case you might have a question or you need help regarding a tutorial, please do not hesitate to reach us at the email address **wirearttutorials@gmail.com**
You can follow us on social media as well:
Instagram: @wirearttutorials
Facebook: Wire Art Tutorials by Erika

Copyright Protection
The whole content of this book, including the pictures and the text, is protected by copyright law. This means that any content of this book cannot be reproduced or cannot be used to offer jewelry making classes. The jewelry made by yourself, following the tutorials of this book, can be used for personal or commercial use as well. Thank you for your understanding!

GETTING STARTED

Wire Wrapping & Weaving Tools

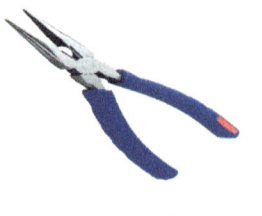
Chain Nose Pliers
Ideal for wire wrapping and shaping, closing jump rings, holding small stones. Outside is rounded and inside has flat facing jaws. Ideal to close the wire ends tightly.

Round Nose Pliers
They are perfect to bend your wire smoothly, to create loops and jump rings, The most used pliers to create multiple jewelry findings.

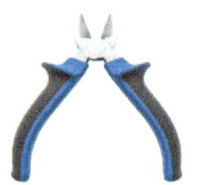
Wire Cutters
They are needed for cutting your wire to the desired length for your jewelry making project.

Bail Making Pliers
They offer 6 size loops on 2 different noses, allowing to bend the wire to make bails and to repeat wire wrapping pattern of the same size each time.

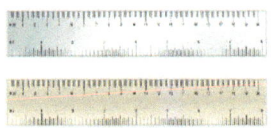
Ruler
Used to measure your wire so you can cut it accurately for your jewelry making projects.

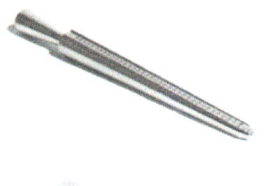
Ring Mandrel
A quick and effortless way to measure your ring size. It is a key part in shaping rings, they are perfect to bend the metal into shape.

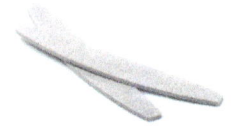
Files (or Sandpaper)
They are particularly useful when we need to smooth down the sharp ends of the wires.

GETTING STARTED

Materials: Wires, Beads

Commonly Used Wires

For our jewelry making projects we can use multiple wires of assorted sizes. We will always use a thicker wire for the base and a thinner wire for the weave. Here is an extremely useful chart to better understand the wire sizes depending on the country where you live.

Gauge	Inches	Millimeters
16	0.052	1.3
18	0.04	1
20	0.032	0.8
21	0.028	0.7
22	0.025	0.6
24	0.02	0.5
26	0.016	0.4
28	0.013	0.3
30	0.01	0.25

Beads

There are multiple types of beads for jewelry making. Commonly used beads for wire jewellery are round, briolette, coin, and tube beads.

Gemstones: Natural and Man-Made

Agate
With a wide variety of colors, they are wonderful, decorative, and extremely popular.

Amazonite
Blue-green and opaque material with an irregular distribution of white materials.

Amber
It is a fossilized plant resin. It can have plants and trapped insects.

Amethyst
It is a quartz. Ranges from very pale through to deep purple color.

GETTING STARTED

Aquamarine
They occur in a range of pale to mid-blues, and they can have pink, green, yellow, white stones.

Chrysocolla
It is a blue-green crystal with high copper content. It has vivid colors, and it is extremely popular in jewelry making.

Citrine (Quartz)
Color ranges from a pale yellow to brown. Citrine and amethyst can be found in the same crystal, which is called ametrine.

Emerald
Is a gemstone and a variety of the mineral beryl. The word Emerald translates to green stone.

Fluorite
It belongs to the halide minerals, and it crystallizes in isometric cubic habit. It is a relatively common mineral.

Garnet
It is associated with a red gemstone however they can occur in many other colors. It is favoured by lapidarists since antient times.

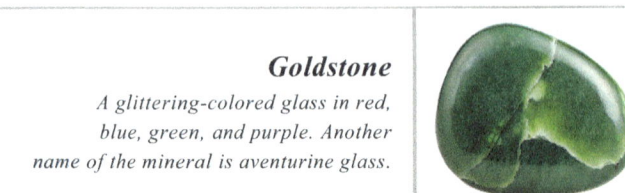

Goldstone
A glittering-colored glass in red, blue, green, and purple. Another name of the mineral is aventurine glass.

Jade
Exist two types: jadeite jade and nephrite jade, both in a range of colors and are very tough materials.

Jasper
It is a patterned variety of quartz, an opaque from chalcedony, often having an abundance of impurities.

Labradorite
It is a feldspar mineral, with colors ranging from purple to grey, blue, green, yellowish, and brown.

Lapis Lazuli
It is an opaque rock which may have white calcite crystals. It usually occurs in crystalline marble.

Malachite
Opaque, bended green copper carbonate mineral. With a patterned surface, it has a rich shade of green.

GETTING STARTED

Moonstone
It is a transparent body with blue adularescence. The most valuable are the transparent ones with strong blue sheen.

Obsidian
It is made from volcanic glass, having a dark colouring. We can differentiate black obsidian and mahogany obsidian.

Opal
A hydrated form of silica, being chemically like quartz. It has a characteristic play of colors which is result of diffraction.

Peridot
It refers to green, gem-quality olivine. It is one of the few gems that occur in only one color: green, from pale green to intense olive green.

Quartz
Is a crystalline and hard mineral composed of silica. Being the most abundant mineral on Earth, it has many varieties.

Rose Quartz
Is has a pale to rich-pink color, with a milky aspect, often faceted to provide a good brilliance.

Sapphire
A transparent to translucent gemstone, ranging from a very pale blue to deep indigo, with the most valued medium-deep cornflower blue.

Spinel
Chemically distinct, very rare gemstone. Available nearly in any color, they are very inviting and sustainable for most types of jewelry.

Topaz
It can occur in distinct colors, being blue to most inexpensive and the highest values go from pink to red.

Tourmaline
Common in most colors, but pure blue, red, orange, and purple are very rare. These crystals are often cracked and flawed.

Turquoise
With an intense sky-blue to blue-green colors, it has been prized by multiple cultures for over 5000 years.

Man-Made: Cubic Zirconia
Called also as lab-grown diamonds. They are made of zirconium dioxide, while diamonds are made from carbon in a natural process.

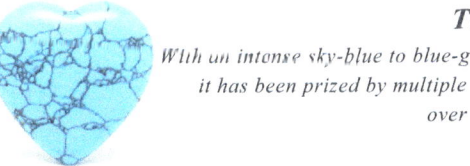

9

GETTING STARTED

Cabochon Shapes

In wire jewelry we can use almost any stone sizes and any stone shapes. In the market we can find an unlimited variety of cabochon shapes, however for beginner wire wrappers I would like to recommend the ones shown below, for having a simpler shape which is easier to be incorporated in wire jewelry designs.

Oval   **Teardrop (Pear)**   **Round**   **Marquise (Horse Eye)**

Which Wire to Use for Wire Wrapping?

When we look to buy wire for jewelry making, we are faced with a wide variety of wires, made with different metals such as copper, sterling silver, fine silver, gold, and some others. All these wires can be found in different hardness, such as dead soft, half hard and hard. Wires might vary in shapes, like round, half round and square wire.

For beginners, it is highly recommended to use dead soft wire, in round shape. The most used wires by beginners are 18ga (1 mm), 20 ga (0.8 mm), 22ga (0.6 mm), 26ga (0.4 mm) and 28ga (0.3 mm) wires. Copper wire is relatively cheaper than precious metals, like silver and gold, therefore it is highly recommended for learning wire jewelry making. Dead soft wire is the most flexible wire, easy to bend it to any direction. It works extraordinarily for wire wrapping jewelry, as it is extremely easy to shape it into spirals and to create free forms, such as loops and swirls. Half hard wire is often used for more stable ring designs and more elaborated, advanced level pendants, as it can be bent into sharp angles, firm shapes, and it gives a solid base to any jewelry.

If we wish to choose silver wire for jewelry making, the most recommended wire is the dead soft sterling silver wire. Fine silver can be too soft to create a solid jewelry, however it still can be used for the weaving wire. For the base wire is highly recommended sterling silver as it has a small amount of copper wire which makes it more consistent once we shape it.

TECHNIQUES

Double Loop Chain / Bracelet

This is a classic technique for a simple and elegant chain for your pendants, necklaces, or it can be used for a bracelet as well. The best wires for this technique are 20ga (0.8 mm) and 18ga (1 mm) wires, Tools needed: round nose pliers, chain nose pliers, wire flush cutter.

1. We will need multiple wire pieces for this chain / bracelet, depending on the length we wish to make it. Each wire piece must be 1 inch (2,5 cm) long. I will use 20ga (0.8 mm) wire.

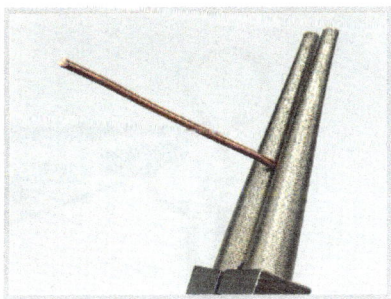

2. Take 1 of these wire pieces, hold the right end of it tight within the center of the round nose pliers, exactly in the same way as shown here.

3. Bend the wire all around the plier, as shown here, to make a closed loop with it.

11

TECHNIQUES

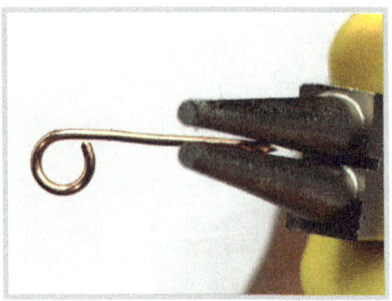 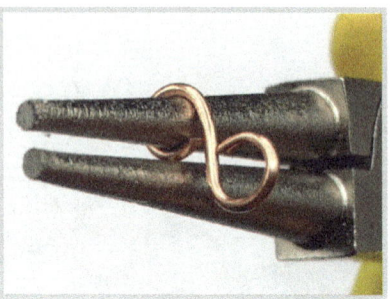 

4. Now hold the other end of the wire tight within the center of the round nose pliers. Make sure that the loop on the left side is pointed downwards.

5. Now bend the wire all around the round nose plier, bending it clockwise until you make another small, closed loop of the same size.

6. Take a second wire, repeat the same bending steps with it, making the second loop of it slightly open, as shown in this picture.

7. Insert the open loop of the second wire into a loop of the first wire, as shown here.

8. With the help of the round nose plier ends, bend this wire end inwards until this loop is completely closed.

9. This is the result we must get. We must check if each loop is completely closed.

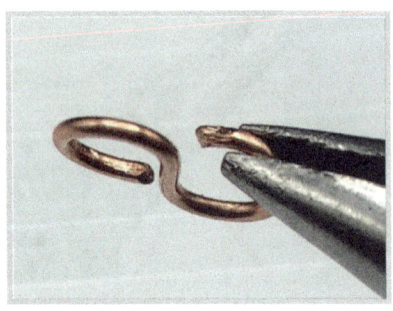 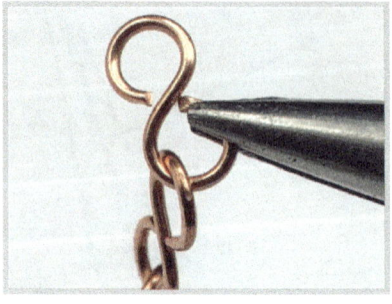 

10. Make another double loop with a third wire, closing both loops. Another way to connect the pieces is: push one loop slightly backwards to open it.

11. Now connect this open loop with the chain you already made, holding it with the chain nose pliers and moving it forward until it is positioned back to its place.

12. We can connect as many wire pieces as we need to complete our chain or bracelet of the desired length.

12

TECHNIQUES

Beaded Loop Chain / Bracelet

A very decorative technique to embellish necklaces with colored beads or to make a gorgeous bracelet for everyday wear. The best wires for this technique are 20ga (0.8 mm) and 18ga (1 mm) wires.
We will need several 4 mm beads for this technique. Tools needed: round nose pliers, chain nose pliers, wire flush cutter.

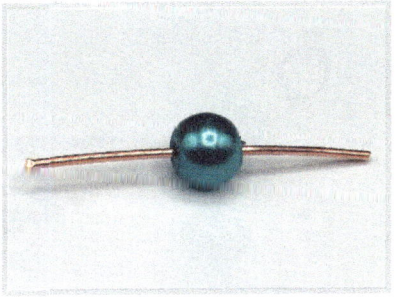

1. We will need multiple wire pieces for this chain / bracelet, depending on the length we wish to make it. Each wire piece must be 1.2 inch (3 cm) long. I will use 20ga (0.8 mm) wire.

2. Take the first wire, add a 4 mm bead to it. We must position this bead over the center of the wire, so both wire ends have the same length.

3. On both sides of the bead bend the wire ends completely upwards as shown here.

TECHNIQUES

4. *On the right side, hold the wire end tight within the center of the round nose pliers.*

5. *With the help of the round nose pliers, bend this wire end clockwise, making a small, closed loop with it on the right side of the bead.*

6. *We must repeat the same steps with the left wire end as well. Hold it tight within the center of the round nose pliers, as shown here,*

7. *With the help of the round nose pliers, bend this wire end counter clockwise, making small, closed loop with it on the left side of the bead.*

8. *This is the result we must get. Both loops must be completely closed near the hole of the bead.*

9. *We must repeat the same steps, to make another beaded wire piece. With the chain nose pliers, push the right loop slightly backwards to open it.*

10. *Connect this open loop with the left loop of the earlier beaded wire piece, as shown here.*

11. *We must close this open loop with the chain nose pliers, moving it forward until it is positioned back to its place, and it is completely closed.*

12. *We can connect as many wire pieces as we need to complete our beaded chain or bracelet of the desired length.*

TECHNIQUES

Loop Chain / Bracelet

It is one of the most versatile techniques, used for chains, bracelets. It can also be an element to connect it with complex pendants. The best wires for this technique are 20ga (0.8 mm) and 18ga (1 mm) wires. Tools needed: round nose pliers, chain nose pliers, wire flush cutter

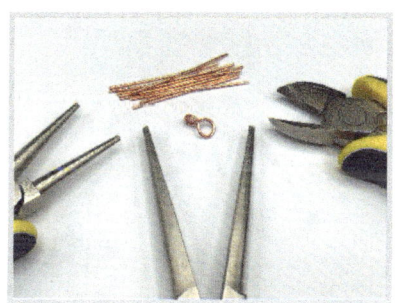

1. We will need multiple wire pieces for this chain / bracelet, depending on the length we wish to make it. Each wire piece must be 1.4 inch (3.5 cm) long. I will use 20ga (0.8 mm) wire.

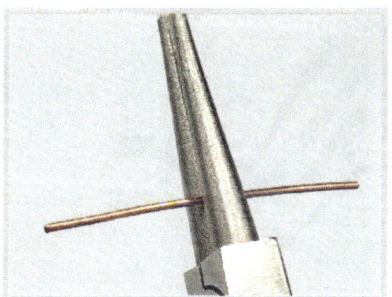

2. Take one of these wires, hold the center of it at a 0.5 cm distance from the bottom of the round nose pliers.

3. Bend the right end of the wire completely to the left side direction, over the upper side of the round nose pliers.

15

TECHNIQUES

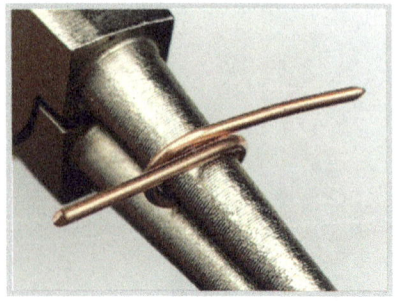

4. *Now bend the left end of the wire completely to the right-side direction, over the upper side of the round nose pliers.*

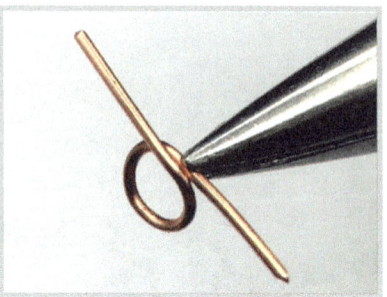

5. *Separate the wire from the pliers. At the top center of the loop, hold the wire end pointed to the right side tight within the ends of the chain nose pliers.*

6. *With the help of the chain nose pliers bend this wire end completely upwards, exactly in the same way as shown here.*

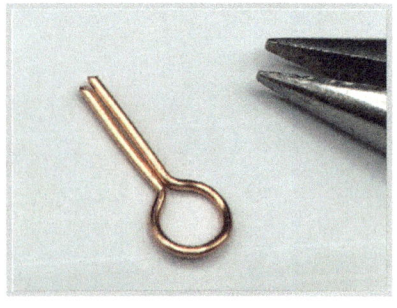

7. *Repeat the same step with the other wire end as well. Both must be pointed upwards and positioned close to each other, as shown here.*

8. *If one wire end is slightly longer than the other one, we must cut off the extra end of it. Both must have the same length.*

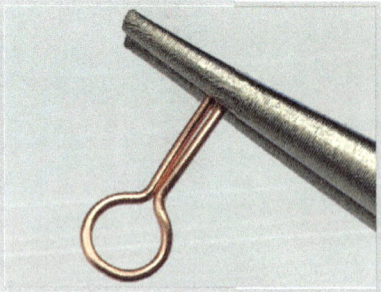

9. *Hold the wire ends tight within the round nose pliers, at an approximately 1 cm distance from the ends of the pliers.*

10. *Hold the loop tight between your fingers, then bend the wire ends backwards with the help of the pliers, making a small open loop with them.*

11. *This is the result we must get. The loops made with the wire ends must stay close to each other.*

12. *With the help of the chain nose pliers, push the wire ends closer to the bent part of the wires, until these small loops are completely closed.*

TECHNIQUES

  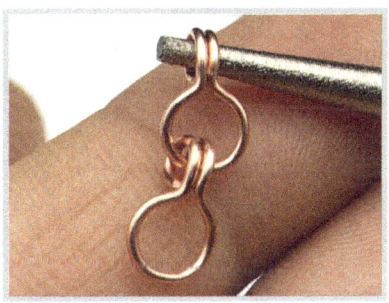

13. *Repeat the same steps with another wire piece, then insert the open loops of it into the front loop of the earlier wire piece, as shown here.*

14. *Again, with the help of the chain nose pliers, push the wire ends closer to the bent part of the wires, until these small loops are completely closed.*

15. *This is the result from the front view we must get when 2 wire pieces are connected.*

16. *We can connect as many wire pieces as we need to complete our chain or bracelet of the desired length.*

17

TECHNIQUES

Chain / Bracelet Closure: Lobster Clasp

Many wire bracelets need a perfect closure for smooth wearing. This clasp lock is one of the popular techniques used by creators. The best wires for this technique are 20ga (0.8 mm) and 18ga (1 mm) wires. Tools needed: round nose pliers, chain nose pliers, wire flush cutter.

1. Cut a 2 inches (5 cm) long wire. I will use 20ga (0.8 mm) wire. Hold the center of it tight within the bottom of the round nose pliers, as shown here.

2. Hold the center of the wire tight within the pliers, then bend the right end of it all around the upper side of the pliers, bending it counter clockwise completely downwards.

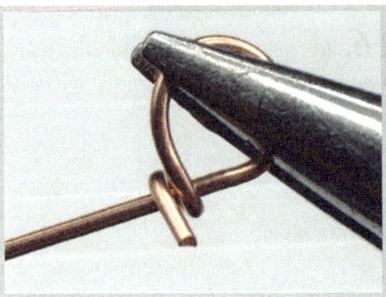

3. Separate it from the round nose pliers. Hold the loop tight within the chain nose pliers, then wrap the shorter wire end once around the longer one.

18

TECHNIQUES

4. Pressure the shorter wire end with the ends of the chain nose pliers, until it is completely closed around the longer wire end.

5. Near the wrapped part, hold the wire within the round nose pliers, at a 0.5 cm distance from the bottom. Bend it around the plier, bending it close to the loop.

6. Insert the bent wire into the last loop of your chain or bracelet, as shown here.

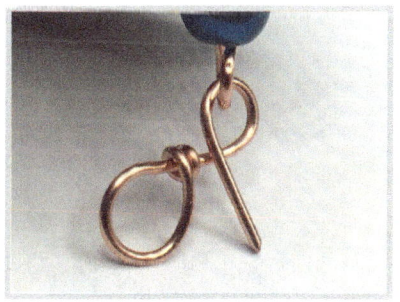

7. Continue to bend the wire end to the other side, making a loop with it, exactly in the same way as shown here.

8. With the help of the chain nose pliers, wrap this wire end around the same wire, as tight as you can.

9. Now pressure the wire end with the chain nose pliers, until it is completely closed.

10. This is the result we must get. This double loop must be positioned on one side of the bracelet, and now we will make the other part of the clasp lock closure.

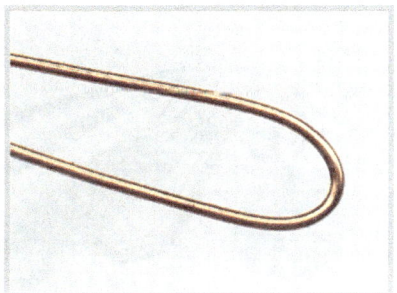

11. Cut a 2.8 inches (7 cm) long wire (use the same wire size as before). Bend it in half, making sure that the wire ends meet on the other end.

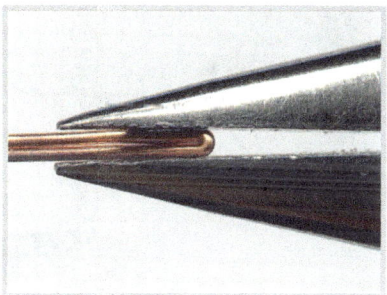

12. With the help of the chain nose pliers, press the center of the wire until it is completely closed, as shown here.

19

TECHNIQUES

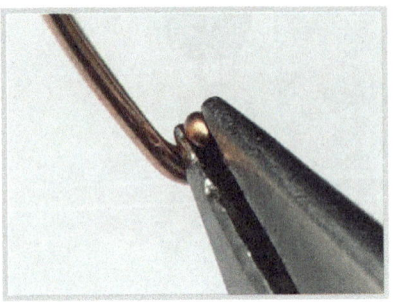

13. *Hold the bent center of the wire tight within the ends of the chain nose pliers, then bend it to the left side direction, to make a very small hook with it.*

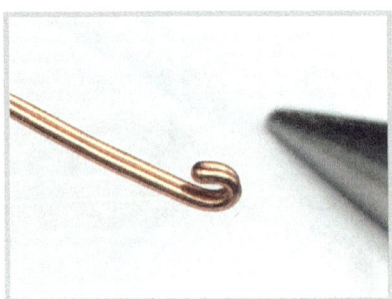

14. *This is the result we must get. This hook must be very small, maximum 0.2 cm tall.*

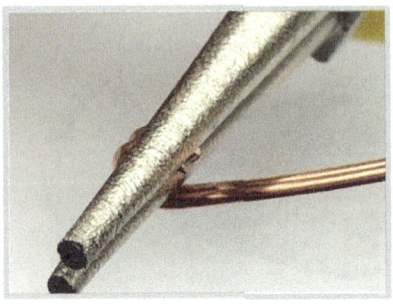

15. *On the left side, hold the wire ends within the center of the round nose pliers. Bend them to the right side, clockwise, making an open loop with them.*

16. *This is the result we must get. These open loops must be a maximum 0.4 cm tall.*

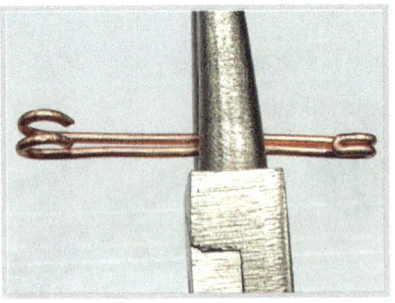

17. *A little bit to the right from the center of the wire, hold it tight within the bottom of the round nose pliers, as shown here.*

18. *Bend both sides of the wire backwards until they almost meet. There must be a very small distance between them, as shown here.*

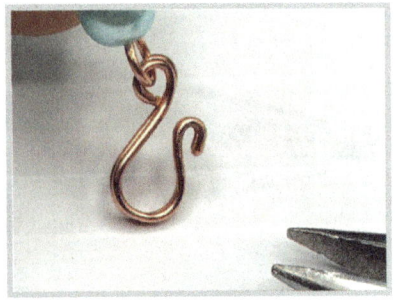

19. *Insert the open loops of the clasp into the loop on the other end of the chain or bracelet. With the chain nose pliers press the small loops of the clasp to close them completely.*

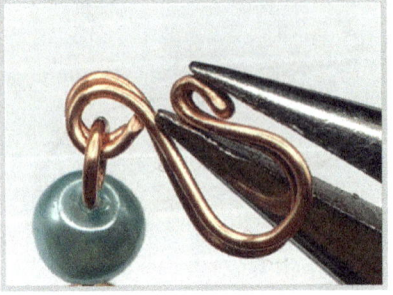

20. *Optional: we can press the small hook of the clasp to close it completely, as shown here.*

21. *This is how the 2 parts of the clasp lock are connected, to have a secure closure for our chain or bracelet.*

TECHNIQUES

Wire Weaving Techniques

Major part of these techniques come from basket weaving which is one of the most antique arts, practiced from strips or fibers of vegetable origin, and of animal origin or human hair and today also from synthetic materials. Wire weaving is creating beautiful patterns by looping a thinner wire around a thicker wire. There are endless possibilities to create wire woven patterns and textures which can be used to embellish any wire jewelry.

Next, I will show you several ways of beginner wire weaving. I recommend you practice with 18ga (1 mm) or 20ga (0.8 mm) wire for the base wire which will be positioned horizontally. For the weave we can use 26ga (0.4 mm), 28ga (0.3 mm) or 30ga (0.25 mm) wires. For all these weaves I will use the combination of 18ga (1 mm) base wires and 26ga (0.4 mm) weaving wires.

To practice these weaving techniques, we will cut 4 inches (10 cm) long base wires. We will always start the weave by positioning the initial end of the weaving wire behind the base wires (close to the left end of the base wires), then we will follow the steps shown. I recommend you weave with your weaving wire from the reel and to cut it off when you decide to stop practicing the weaving around the base wires.

Very important!
1. Before starting any weave, always make sure that the base wires are completely straight, otherwise straighten them as much as possible.
2. Always make sure that the base wires used in the specific weave are aligned on both sides.

1. Weaving around 2 base wires: 2-1 weave

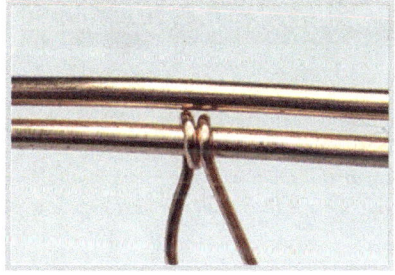 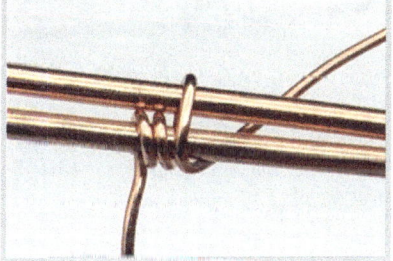 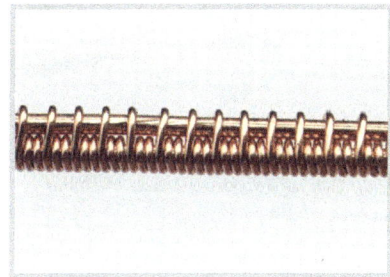

Wrap the weaving wire 2 times around the lower base wire.

Wrap it once around both base wires, as tight as you can.

Repeat the same weaving steps multiple times. This is the result we must get.

2. Weaving around 2 base wires: 3-1 weave

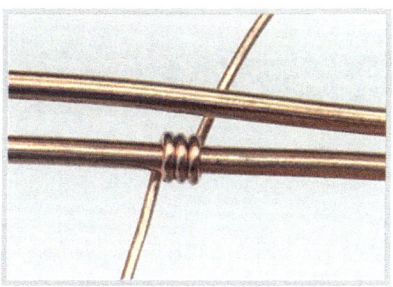 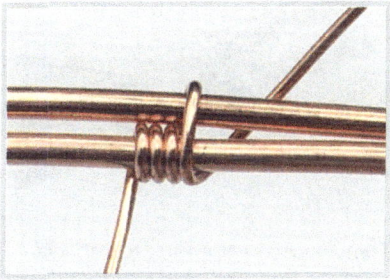 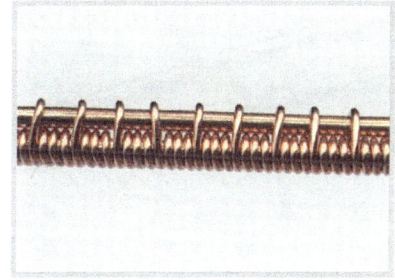

Wrap the weaving wire 3 times around the lower base wire.

Wrap it once around both base wires, as tight as you can.

Repeat the same weaving steps multiple times. This is the result we must get.

21

TECHNIQUES

3. *Weaving around 2 base wires: 3-2 weave*

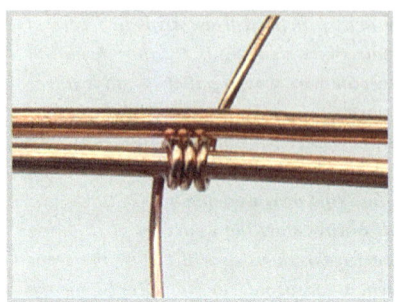
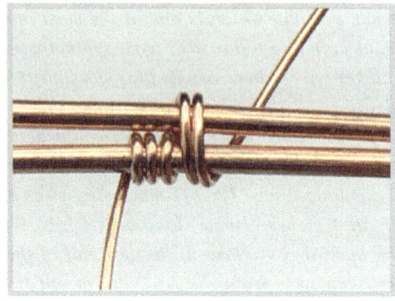
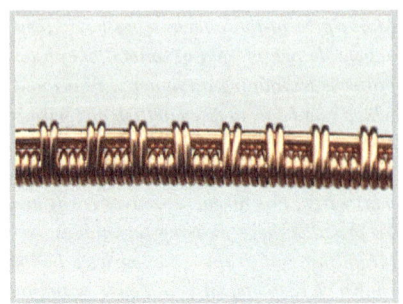

Wrap the weaving wire 3 times around the lower base wire.

Wrap it 2 times around both base wires, as tight as you can.

Repeat the same weaving steps multiple times. This is the result we must get.

4. *Weaving around 2 base wires: 5-2 weave*

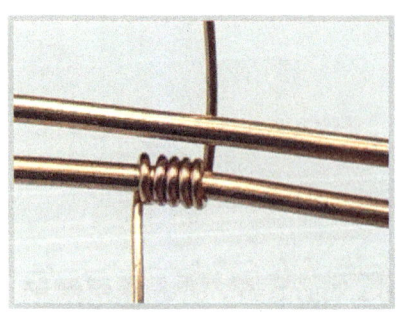
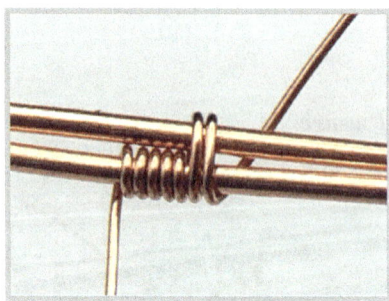
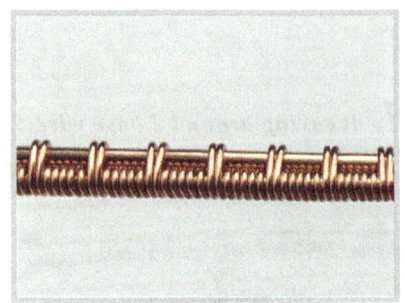

Wrap the weaving wire 5 times around the lower base wire.

Wrap it 2 times around both base wires, as tight as you can.

Repeat the same weaving steps multiple times. This is the result we must get.

5. *Weaving around 2 base wires: simplified figure 8 weave*

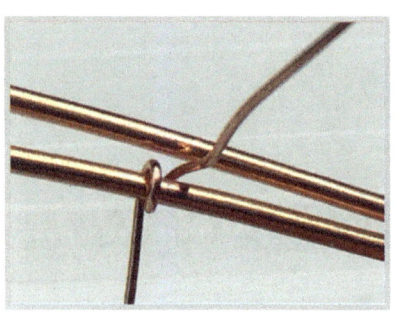
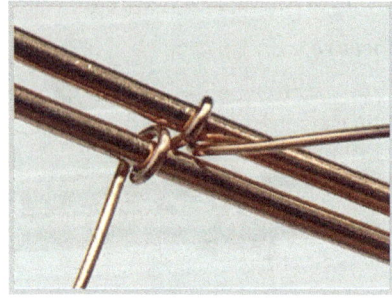
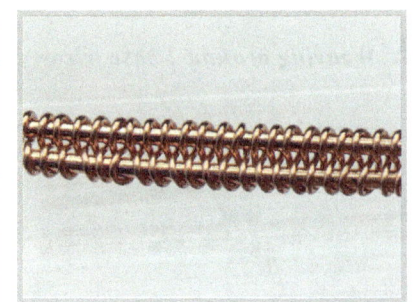

Wrap the weaving wire once around the lower base wire, then take it to the front between these 2 base wires.

Wrap the weaving wire once around the upper base wire, then take it to the front between these 2 base wires.

Repeat the same weaving steps multiple times. This is the result we must get.

TECHNIQUES

6. Weaving around 2 base wires: classic figure 8 weave

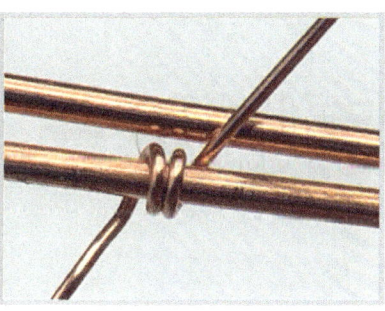
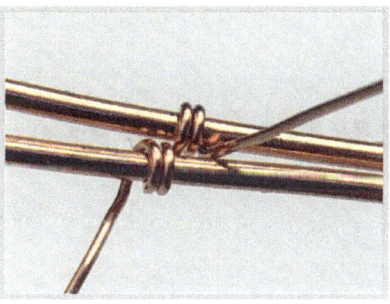
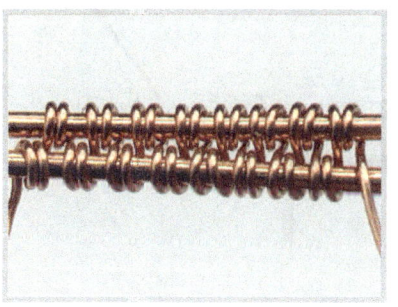

Wrap the weaving wire 2 times around the lower base wire, then take it to the front between these 2 base wires.

Wrap the weaving wire 2 times around the upper base wire, then take it to the front between these 2 base wires.

Repeat the same weaving steps multiple times. This is the result we must get.

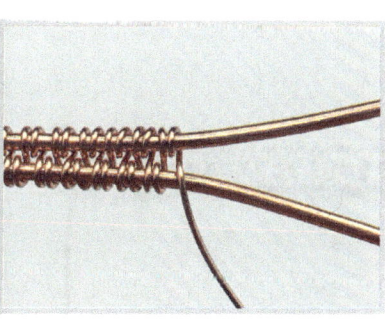
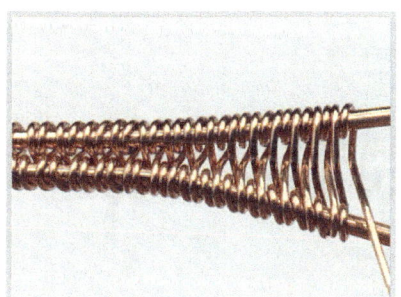

Continue to weave around the base wires, following the same weaving steps and keeping the distance between the base wires. This figure 8 weave is one of the most embellishing weaves used for more elaborated wire wrapped pendant designs and bails.

Now we can test how this weave looks when we separate the base wires a little bit.

7. Weaving around 2 base wires: 2-1 zigzag weave

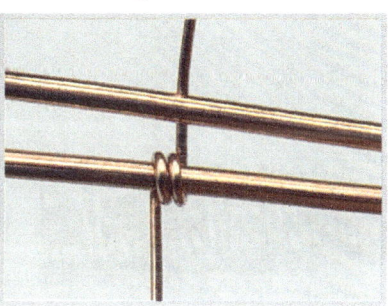
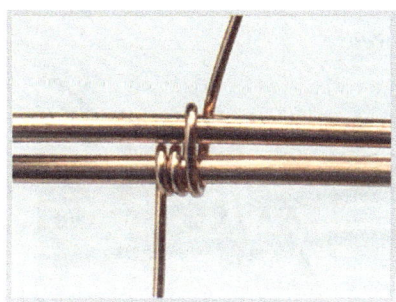
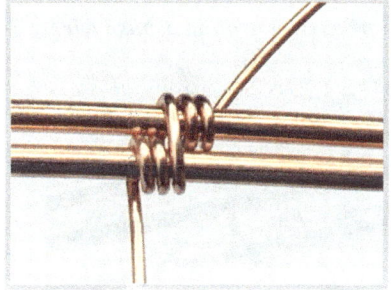

Wrap the weaving wire 2 times around the lower base wire.

Wrap it once around both base wires, as tight as you can.

Now wrap the weaving wire 2 times around the upper base wire.

23

TECHNIQUES

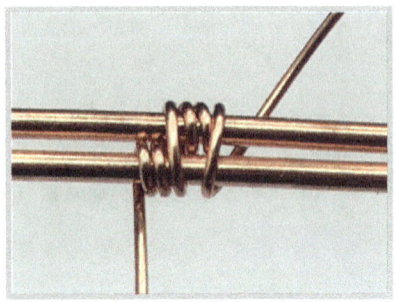

Make another tight wrap around both base wires, to finish 1 rotation of this weave.

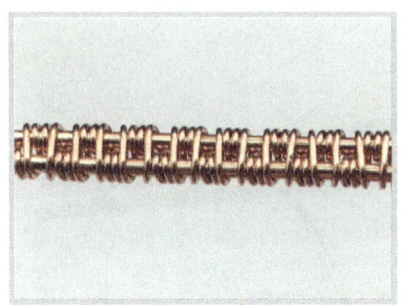

Repeat the same weaving steps multiple times. This is the result we must get.

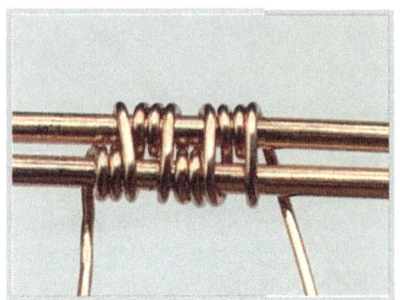

I will show you how this weave looks when it is compressed. Make 2 rotations of the same weaving steps, as shown.

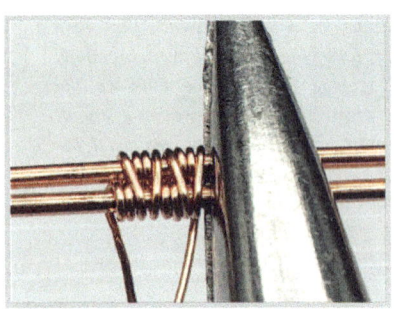

With the help of the chain nose pliers, push the woven wires to the left side direction, until it is compressed.

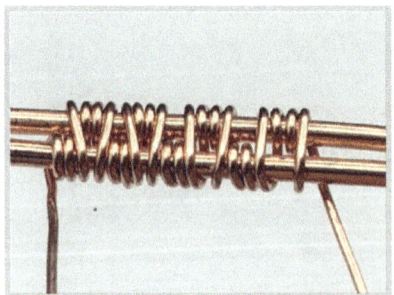

Once it is compressed, make another 2 rotations of this weave.

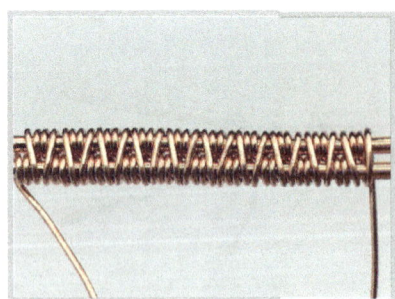

Repeat the same weaving steps, compressing it after every 2 rotations, to obtain the result shown here.

8. Weaving around 3 base wires: 3-2 weave

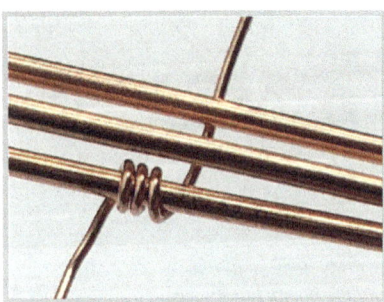

Wrap the weaving wire 3 times around the lower base wire.

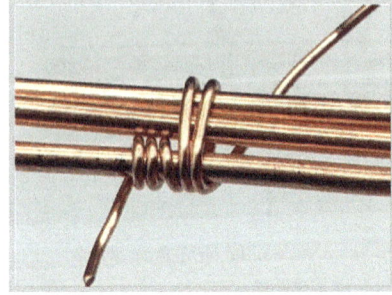

Wrap it 2 times around all the 3 base wires, as tight as you can.

Repeat the same weaving steps multiple times. This is the result we must get.

TECHNIQUES

9. *Weaving around 3 base wires: 1-1 zigzag weave*

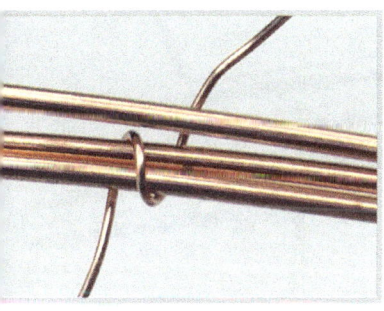 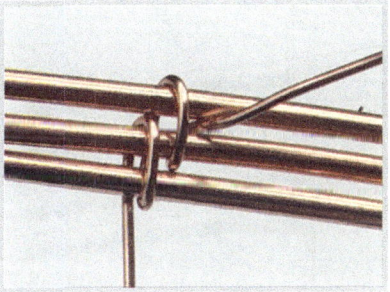 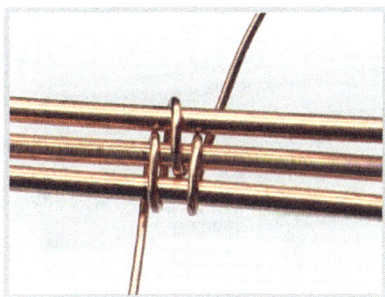

Wrap the weaving wire once around the 2 lower base wires.

Now wrap it once around the 2 upper base wires, then take it to the front between these 2 wires.

Again, wrap the weaving wire once around the 2 lower base wires, as tight as you can.

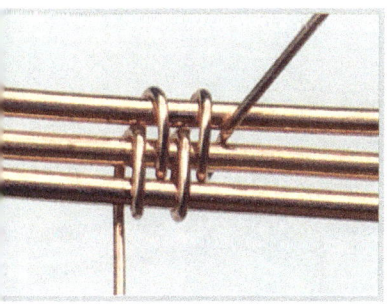 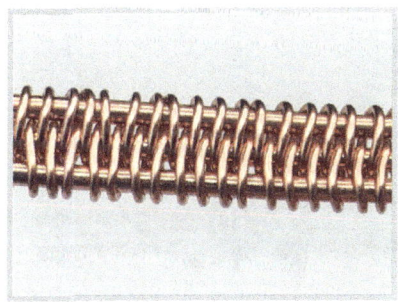

Now wrap it once around the 2 upper base wires, to finish the second rotation of this weave.

Repeat the same weaving steps multiple times. This is the result we must get.

10. *Weaving around 3 base wires: 3-1 central weave*

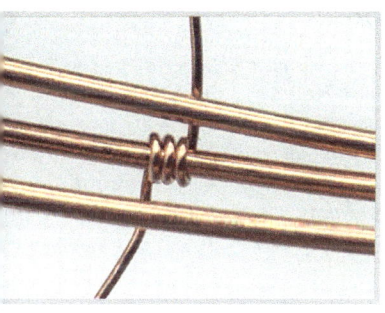 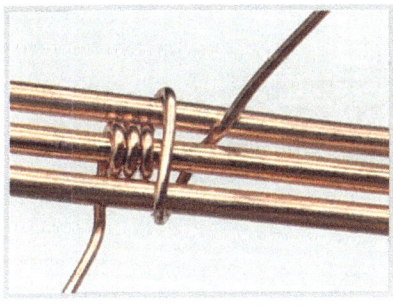 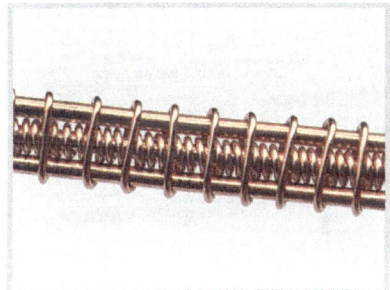

Wrap the weaving wire 3 times around the central base wire, as shown.

Now wrap it once around all the 3 base wires, to connect them tightly.

Repeat the same weaving steps multiple times. This is the result we must get.

25

TECHNIQUES

11. Weaving around 4 base wires: Sun weave

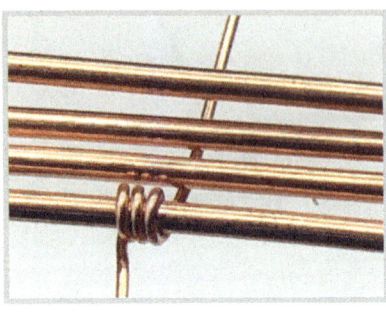

Wrap the weaving wire 3 times around the lower base wire, as tight as you can.

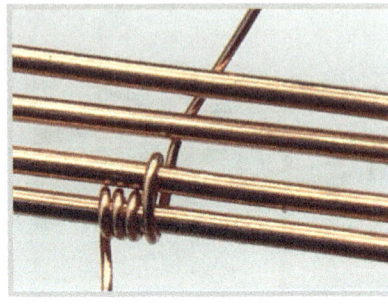

Wrap it once around the 2 bottom wires.

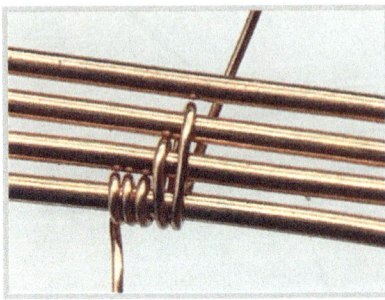

Now make a tight wrap around the 3 bottom wires.

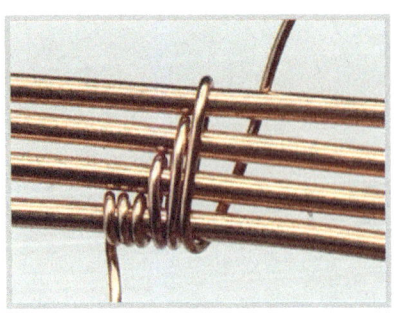

Wrap the weaving wire once around all the 4 base wires, as tight as you can.

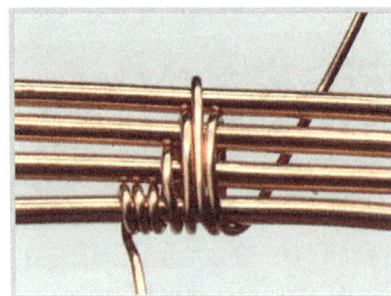

Now make a wrap around the 3 bottom wires.

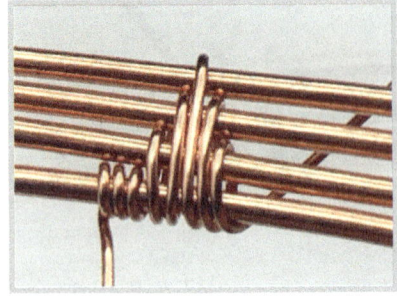

Wrap the weaving wire once around the 2 bottom wires.

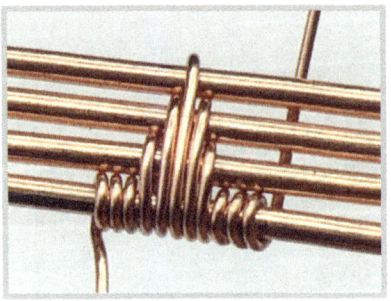

Now again wrap the weaving wire 3 times around the lower base wire, as shown.

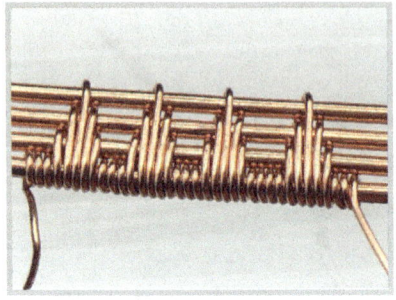

Repeat the same weaving steps multiple times. This is the result we must get.

TIP:

This weave can be experimented with mor than 4 base wires as well, as many as yo wish. Each time we will weave upwards firs increasing the number of base wires involve in each wrap, then we will wea downwards, decreasing the base wir involved in each wrap.

26

TECHNIQUES

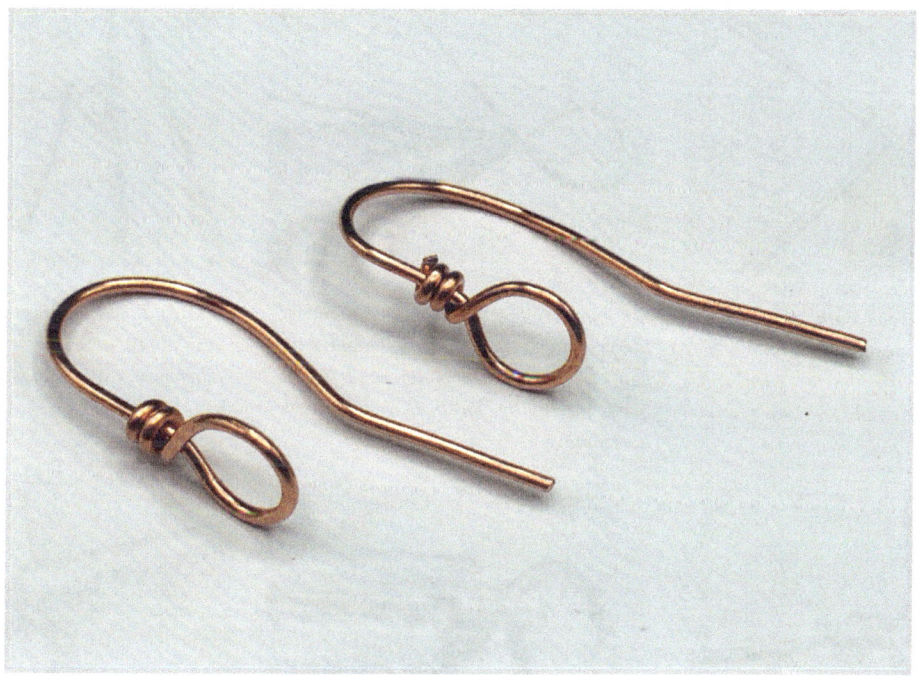

Ear Wires for Earrings

There are multiple styles of ear wires we can create. This time I will teach you how to make ear wires with a hook that connect with the earrings part. The best wires for this technique are 20ga (0.8 mm) and 18ga (1 mm) wires. Tools needed: round nose pliers, chain nose pliers, wire flush cutter, nail file.

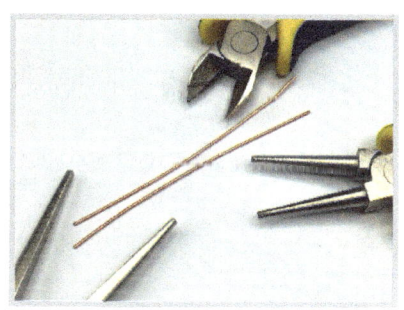

1. Cut 2 wires with the length of 3 inches (7,5 cm), each. I will use 20ga (0.8 mm) wire.

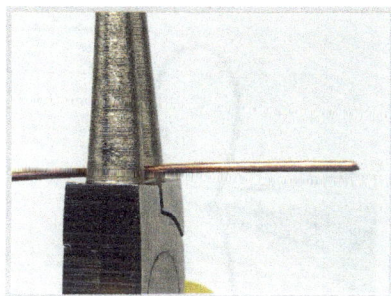

2. Take one of these wires. On the right end of it measure 1,5 cm, then hold it tight within the bottom of the round nose pliers, as shown.

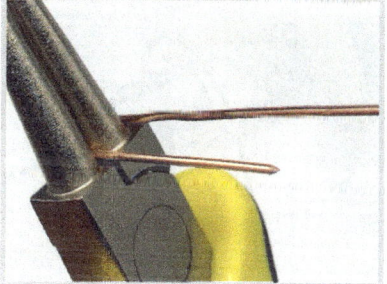

3. Bend the longer end of this wire completely to the right-side direction, bending it tightly around the upper side of the round nose pliers.

27

TECHNIQUES

4. *Continue to bend both ends of this wire to the opposite directions, as shown, bending the shorter wire end over the longer wire end.*

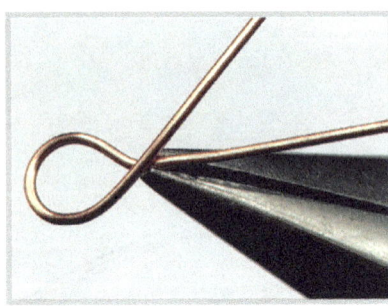

5. *Separate the wire from the pliers. At the crossing point, hold the longer wire end tight within the chain nose pliers, bend it slightly upwards, to make it horizontal.*

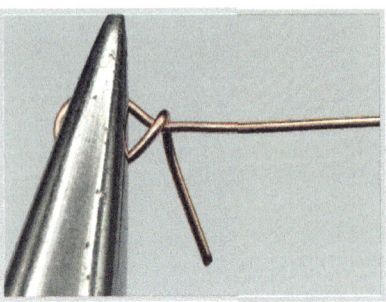

6. *Hold the loop tight within the chain nose pliers, as shown. Start to wrap the shorter wire end around the longer one, as tight as you can.*

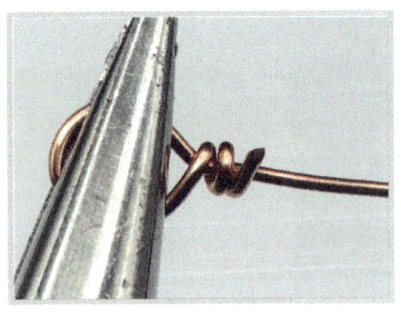

7. *Wrap the short wire end around the longer one until you arrive close to the end of it.*

8. *Now press the wrapped wire end with the chain nose pliers, until it is completely closed, as shown.*

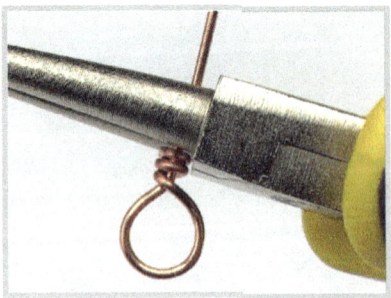

9. *Above the recently wrapped part, hold the longer wire end tight within the bottom of the round nose pliers, completely.*

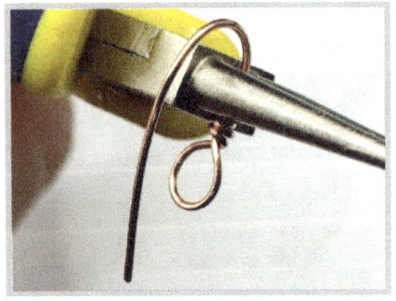

10. *Switch to the back view and bend the wire end downwards, making a hook with it, exactly in the same way as shown here.*

11. *Measure maximum 1 cm on the wire end, at this point hold it with the chain nose pliers and bend it slightly downwards, to make it vertical.*

12. *Repeat the same steps to create a second ear wire. With the help of a nail file, gently file the wire ends, to make them smooth.*

TECHNIQUES

Making Loops

Loops can be extremely decorative in wire jewelry and there are endless ways to incorporate them into our designs. They are a good option to finish the wire ends of a pendant, to add embellishments to it, or to create bead settings. We can practice making loops with a piece of 20ga (0.8 mm) wire (4 inches / 10 cm long). Tools we need: round nose pliers, chain nose pliers.

Open and Closed Circular Loops (Swirls)

1. Take a short wire (4 inches/ 10 cm long). Hold the right end of it tight within the ends of the round nose pliers, as shown.

2. With the help of the round nose pliers, bend the wire end to the left side direction, making a very small open loop with it.

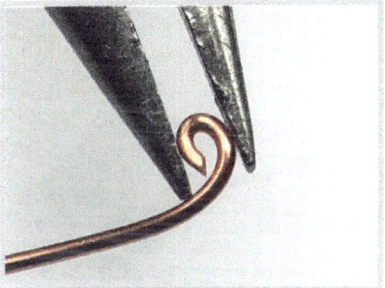

3. Pressure this small open loop with the chain nose pliers to close it completely, as shown here.

TECHNIQUES

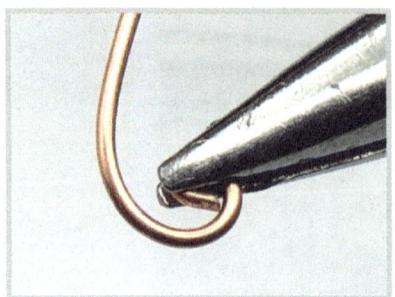

4. Hold this loop within the ends of the chain nose pliers. Continue to bend the wire clockwise, leaving a little space between the loop and the bent part.

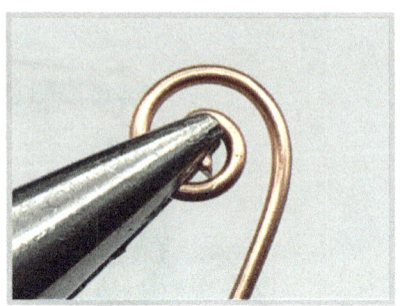

5. Now hold the recently bent part tight within the chain nose pliers and continue to bend the wire downwards, as shown.

6. We can bend the wire end as much as we wish, making this open swirl bigger and bigger.

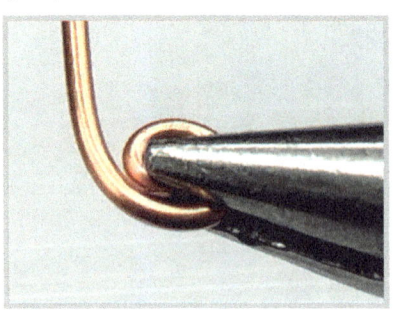

7. Repeat the steps 1-2-3 with another wire piece. Next, hold the small loop tight within the chain nose pliers, then continue to bend it tightly, as shown.

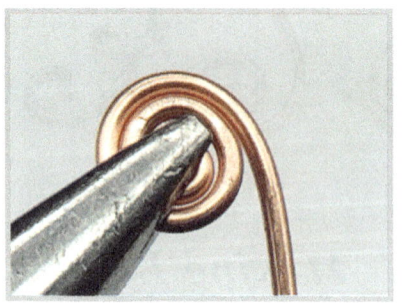

8. Hold the left side of the tight loops with the chain nose pliers and continue to bend the wire end very closely around the loops.

9. We can continue to bend the wire end as much as we wish, making this closed and tight swirl bigger and bigger.

Loop After Loop

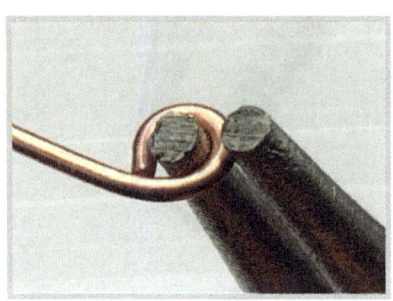

1. Take a 4 inches/ 10 cm long wire. With the tip of the round nose pliers, bend the right wire end inwards, making a closed loop.

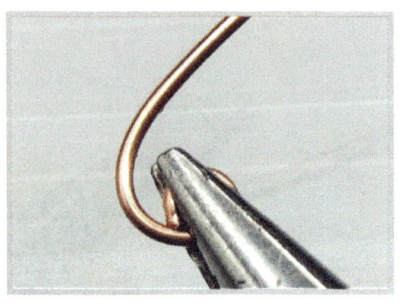

2. Hold this loop within the ends of the chain nose pliers. Bend the wire upwards, leaving a little space between the loop and the bent part.

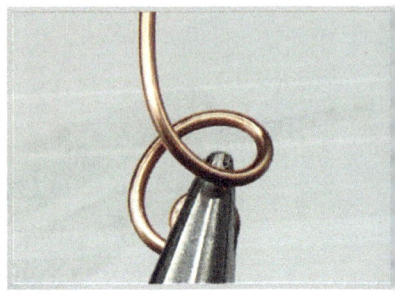

3. Bend the wire to make a loop with it, as shown here.

30

TECHNIQUES

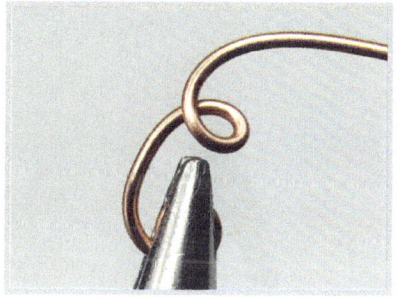
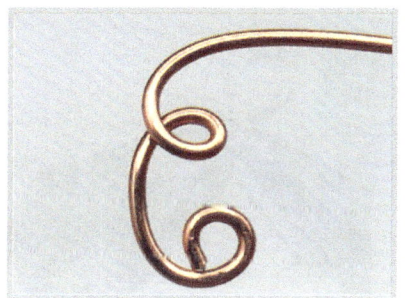

4. Pull the wire end to tighten this loop, making it smaller as much as we like it.

5. This is the result we get. We can make more and more loops after each other, following the same steps.

Bead Setting with Loops

1. Cut a wire which has 1 inch (2,5 cm) length on both sides of the bead, positioning the bead over the center of the wire. My bead is 15 mm tall.

2. Bend the lower wire end to the right-side direction, as shown here.

3. Hold the upper wire end with the ends of the chain nose pliers, bend it slightly to the left side, as shown.

4. Hold the upper wire end within the center of the round nose pliers, then bend it to the opposite direction around the plier, as shown.

5. Continue to bend this wire end to the left side, making a loop around the plier.

6. This is the result we must get. The lower wire end is pointed to the right side, on the upper side we have a small loop at the top of the bead.

31

TECHNIQUES

7. Hold the top loop tight within the chain nose pliers, then bend the short wire end around the bottom of this loop.

8. Press the wire end with the chain nose pliers until it is completely closed.

9. This is the result we must get at the top of the bead. Make sure that the wire end is completely closed.

10. On the lower side, close to the hole of the bead, hold the wire tight within the ends of the round nose pliers, bend it counter clockwise.

11. Now pull the wire slowly with your fingers, making a very small loop with it, as shown.

12. We must continue to bend the wire end around the small loop, as tight as possible.

13. Once we arrive close to the end of the wire, we can bend it with the help of the chain nose pliers, as shown here.

14. With the chain nose pliers, push the short wire end closer to the loop, until it is completely closed and hidden. The bead setting is ready.

I hope you enjoyed these techniques. Feel free to experiment making loops with different bead sizes and shapes.

TUTORIALS

Classy Bead Ring

Rings exist since early humankind. In early Rome the first rings were made in iron and gold, symbolizing the social status of everyone. Wearing a gold ring was restricted to certain classes. In Egypt handcrafted ring were found in the tombs, and the ancient Greeks wore rings simply for decoration.
Today we wear rings simply as adornment or as symbol of marital fidelity. The traditional ring types have mostly disappeared, giving space to all kinds of rings inspired by past styles.

In this very simple tutorial, we will learn how to set a small bead into an elegant and classy ring.
Tools needed: chain (or flat) nose pliers, round nose pliers, wire flush cutter, ring mandrel (or wooden dowel)
Wires: -18ga (1 mm): 1x 12 inches (30 cm)
       -26ga (0.4 mm) wire: 1x 3 inches (7.5 cm)
       -round bead between 4- 6 mm big (I will use a 6 mm big bead)

TUTORIALS

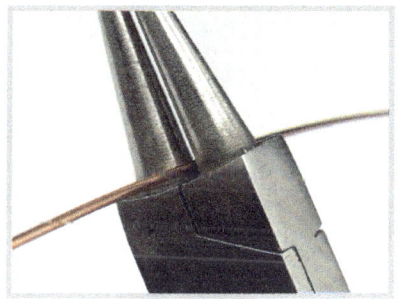

1. Cut a 12 inches (30 cm) long wire of the 18ga (1 mm) wire. Hold the center of it tight between the bottom of the round nose pliers.

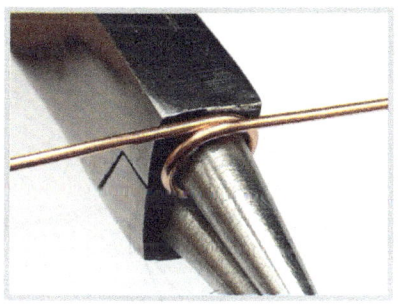

2. Bend both ends of the wire all around the upper side of the round nose pliers, as shown here.

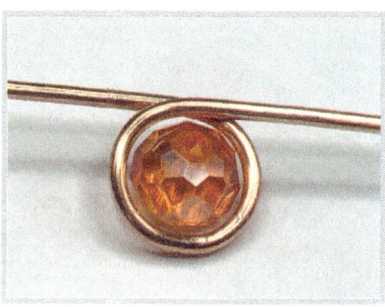

3. Separate the wire from the pliers, then position your bead inside the loop. Make sure that it fits in the loop, otherwise adjust the size of it.

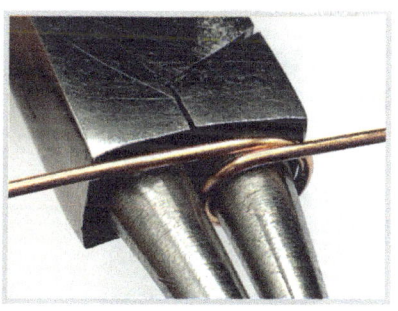

4. We must position the loop on the right side of the round nose pliers in a way that the 2 ends of the wire are on the top.

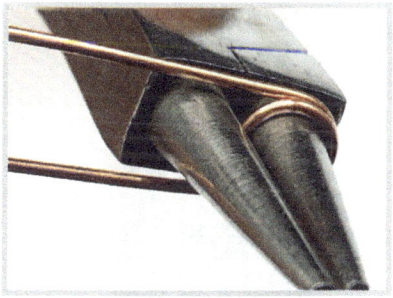

5. Take the wire end from the right side, bend it completely to the opposite direction under the round nose plier, as tight as you can.

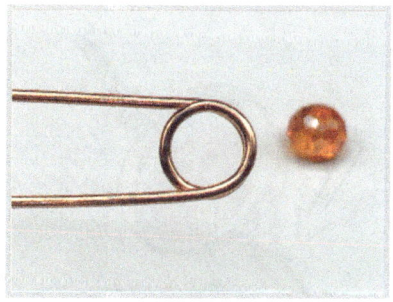

6. This is the result we must get. In this small loop we will insert the bead later.

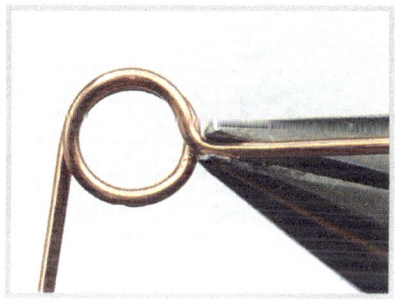

7. Position the wire ends of the loop pointed downwards. On the right center of the loop, hold the wire end tight within the chain nose pliers and bend to the right side.

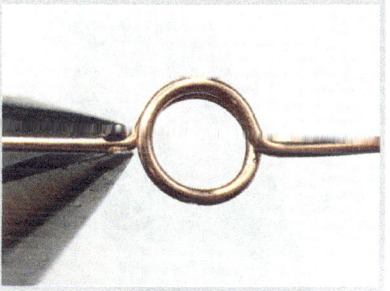

8. We must repeat the same step on the left side as well, bending the wire end to the left side direction, making it horizontal and symmetrical with the other wire end.

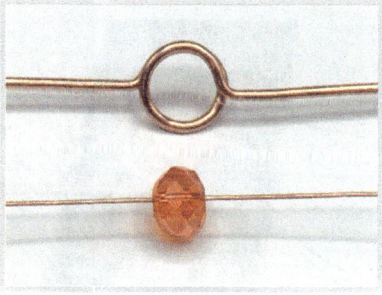

9. Cut a 3 inches (7.5 cm) long wire of the 26ga (0.4 mm) wire. Position it inside the hold of the bead, positioning the bead over the center of this thin wire.

TUTORIALS

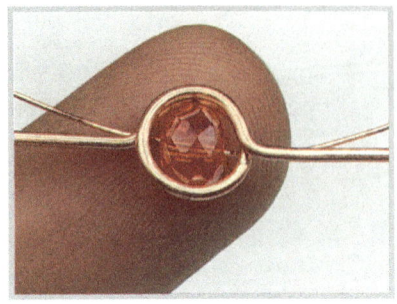

10. Position the loop of the wire structure over the bead, exactly in the same way as shown here. The weaving wire with the bead behind the base wire.

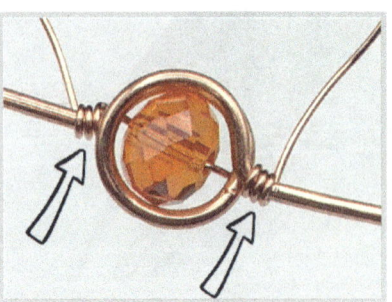

11. On both sides of the bead, at the bent corners of the base wires, wrap the weaving wire ends 3 times around the base wires, as shown with the arrows.

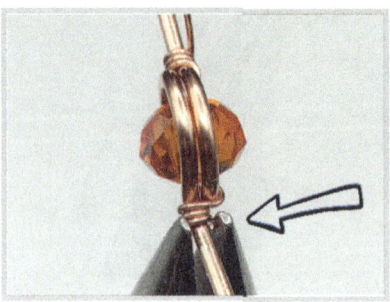

12. On the right side, cut off the extra weaving wire end. With the help of the chain nose pliers, press the short end of it, until it is completely closed.

13. We must repeat the same steps on the left side as well. Make sure that the weaving wire ends are completely closed as we do not want to be able to feel them.

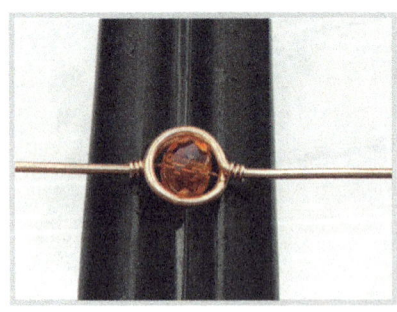

14. Position the beaded center of the base wire over the ring mandrel, over the size you wish the ring to be.

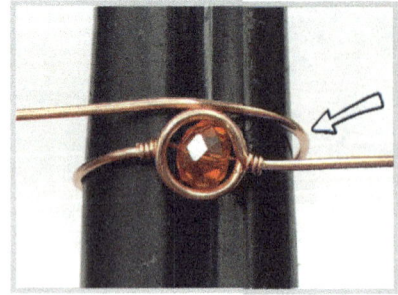

15. Bend the left wire end all around the ring mandrel, as tight as you can, bending it to the front above the beaded part.

16. Now bend the right wire end all around the ring mandrel, as tight as you can, bending it to the front below the beaded part.

17. Continue to bend both wire ends around the mandrel until they are bent to the opposite directions on the back of it, as shown with the arrows.

18. Very slowly, separate the ring from the mandrel. Pay attention not to move the bent wires, to keep the shape of them, as shown here.

TUTORIALS

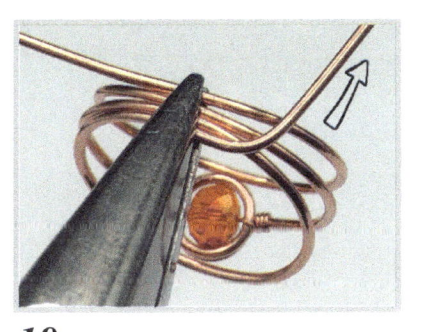

19. Switch to the back view. On the center of the back, hold all wires tight between your fingers or the chain nose pliers, then bend the right wire end upwards.

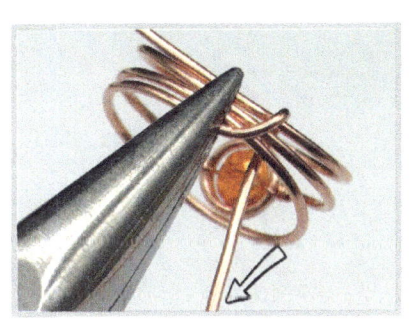

20. Keep holding the wires tightly, then bend the wire end completely downwards behind these wires.

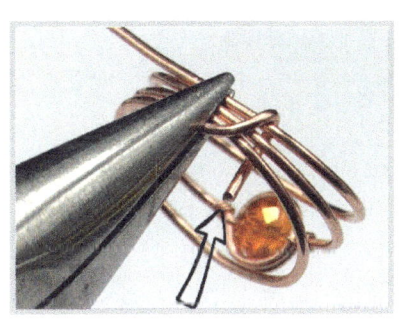

21. Leave a 0.5 cm long end on this wire, cut off the extra end of it.

22. With the help of the chain nose pliers, bend this short wire end completely upwards over the wires, then press it until it is completely closed.

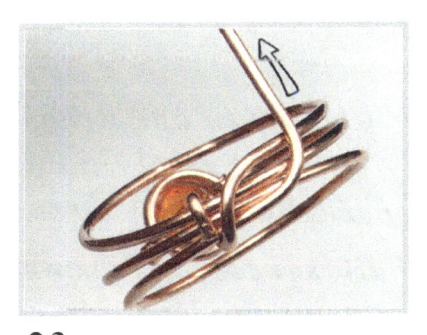

23. We must turn the ring upside down as we have to repeat the same steps on the other side with the other base wire end.

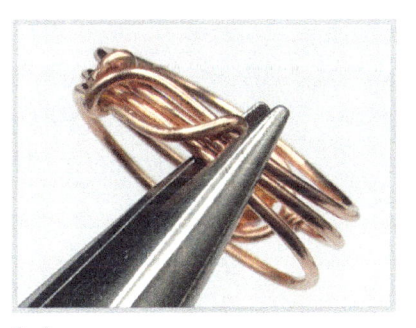

24. After the wire end is bent around the horizontal wires, cut off the extra end of it, then bend it upwards and press it with the chain nose pliers until it is completely closed.

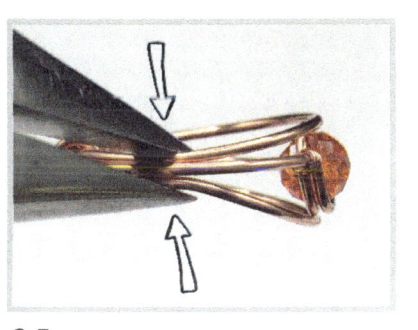

25. On the left side of the ring, press the wires with your fingers or with the help of the chain nose pliers, to position them closer to each other.

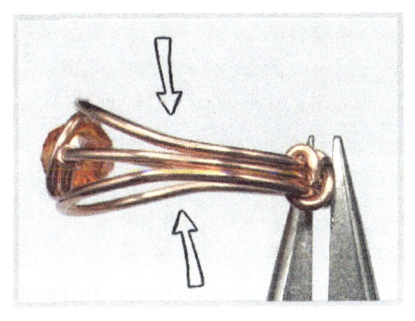

26. We must repeat the same step on the right side of the ring as well.

27. Your beautiful ring is ready.

TIP: Try to use a larger bead for an eye-catching result. Use silver wire to get a brighter and very elegant ring.

37

Tip:

Complex designs like woven and wrapped wire can be a challenge to clean. Here's a great tip to clean tarnish from copper wire and sheet.

Cut a lemon in half, squeeze the lemon juice in a glass. Insert your jewelry inside the lemon juice and let it stay for at least 1 minute. Rinse your jewelry with warm water and dry thoroughly. Your copper jewelry is bright and shining again.

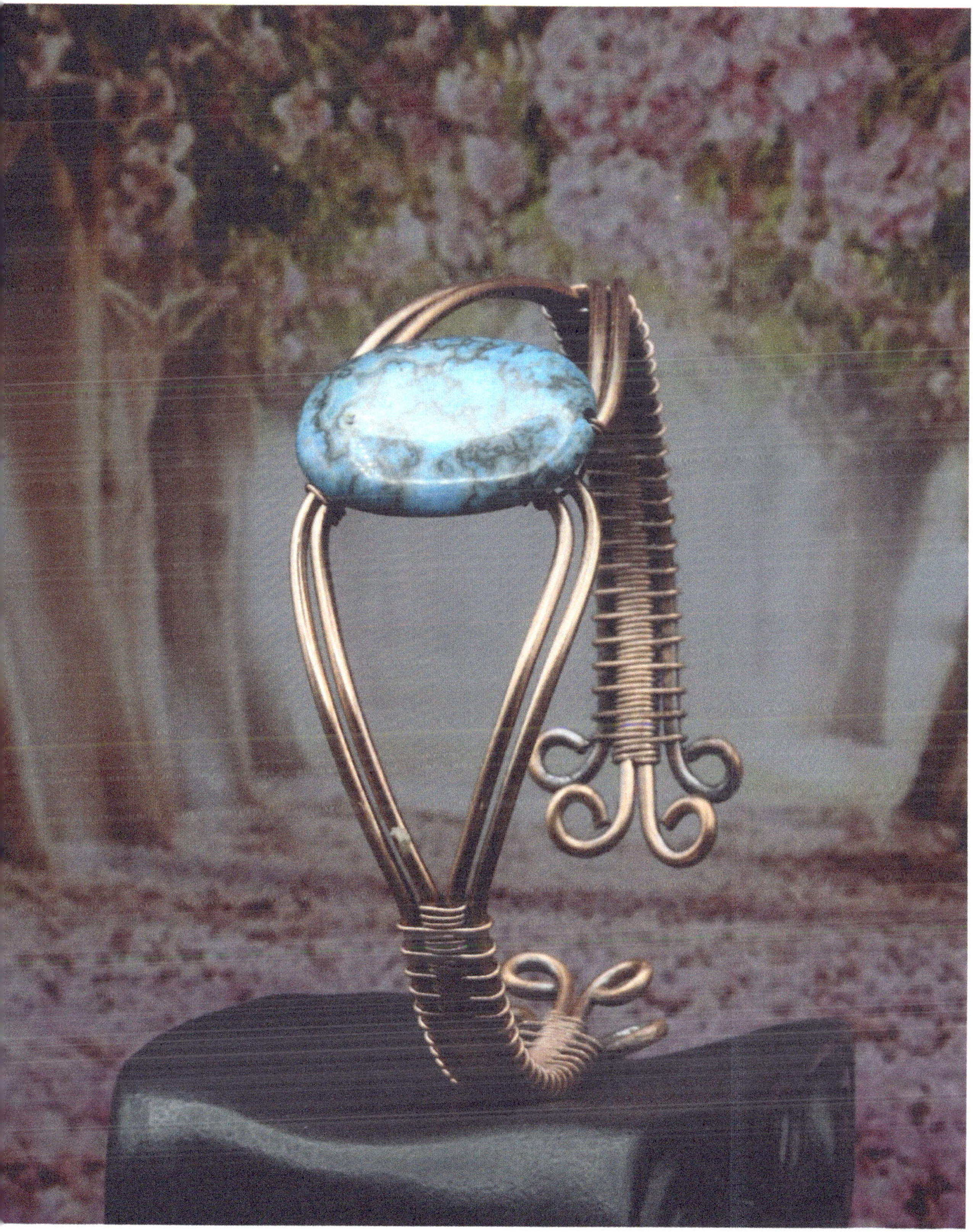

TUTORIALS

Egyptian Bracelet

Ancient Egyptians made incredibly beautiful bracelets and armlets, using precious metals such as gold, and gemstones, like lapis lazuli, malachite, amethyst, turquoise and carnelian, etc. They thought that the more jewelry they wore, the more attractive they would be to the gods. Everyone wore jewelry in ancient Egypt, from poor farmers to wealthy royals. For the wealthy, pieces were made from semi-precious stones, precious metals, and glass beads. The poor substituted these with painted clay, stones, shells, animal teeth and bones.
In this project we will learn how to make an elegant and decorated bracelet.
Tools needed: chain (or flat) nose pliers, round nose pliers, wire cutter
Wires: -18ga (1 mm) OR 17ga (1.25 mm) wire: 4x 8 inches (20 cm)
  -26ga (0.4 mm) wire: 1x 20 inches (50 cm), 2x 72 inches (80 cm)
  -oval shaped bead of 20 mm tall

40

TUTORIALS

1. Materials and tools for this project are shown on this picture. I will use 17ga (1.25 mm) base wire, 26ga (0.4 mm) weaving wire, and a beautiful 20 mm tall Ripple Jasper.

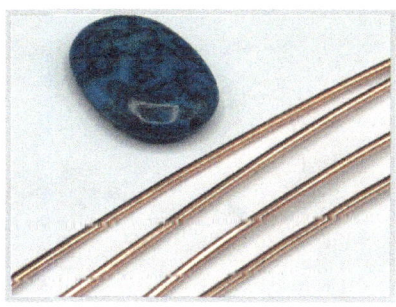

2. Cut 4 base wires with the length of 8 inches (20 cm), each.

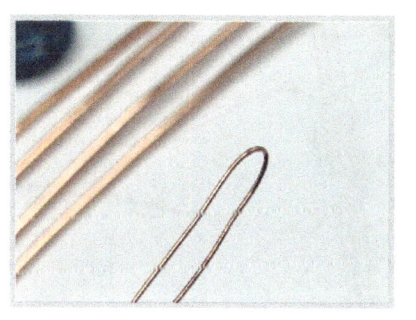

3. Cut a 20 inches (50 cm) long weaving wire of the 26ga (0.4 mm) wire. Bend it in half, as shown here.

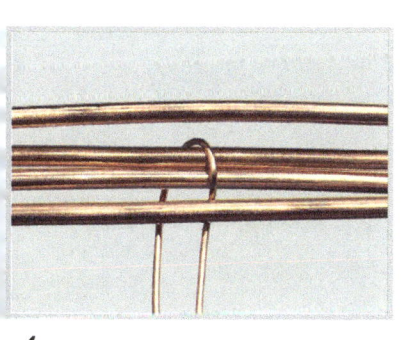

4. Hold the base wires together, making sure that the ends of them are aligned. Position the center of the weaving wire around the center of the inner base wires.

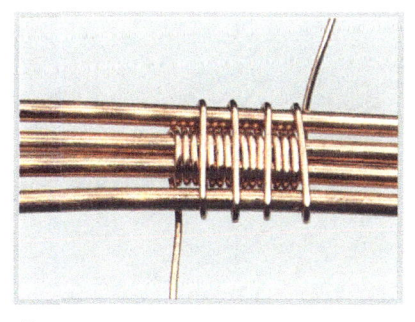

5. With the front end of the weaving wire, make 4 rotations of the 3-1 central weave, as tight as possible, as shown here.

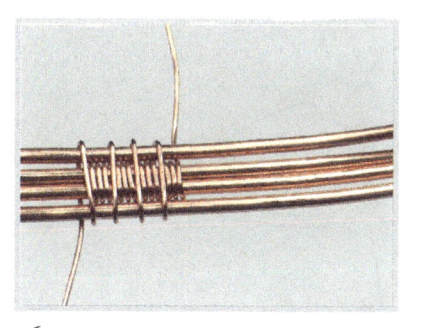

6. Turn the wire structure from the right side to the left side, clockwise. In this way the recently woven part is on the left side of the base wires.

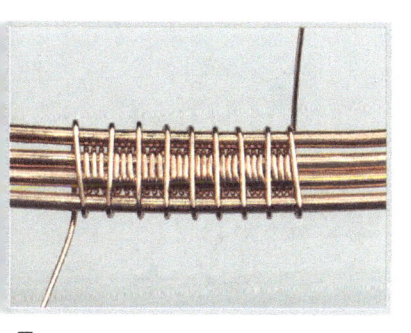

7. Take the other end of the weaving wire, wrap it once around all 4 base wires, then make 4 rotations of the 3-1 central weave, as we did on the other side before.

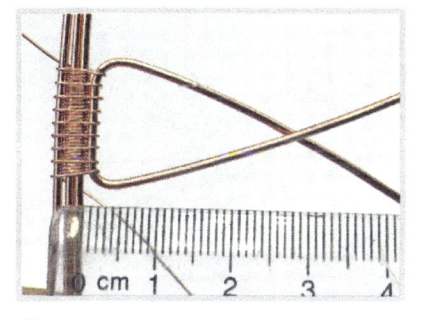

8. Position the wire structure in vertical. Bend the 2 ends of the right base wire to the right side, until they cross over each other at a 3 cm distance from the woven part.

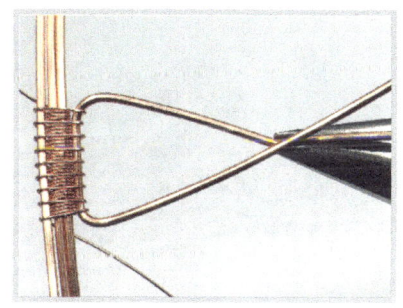

9. At this point where the wire ends meet, hold the upper wire end tight within the tip of the chain nose pliers and straighten it, to make it horizontal.

41

TUTORIALS

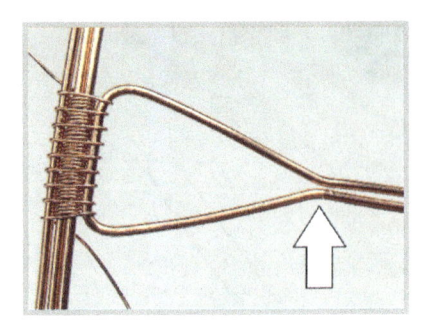

10. Repeat the same step with the lower wire end as well, making them both horizontals.

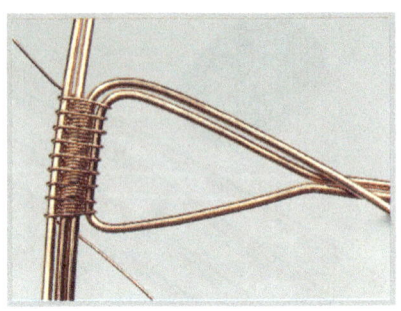

11. Take the next wire end from the upper side, bend it downwards, bending it close to the previously bent base wire, as shown.

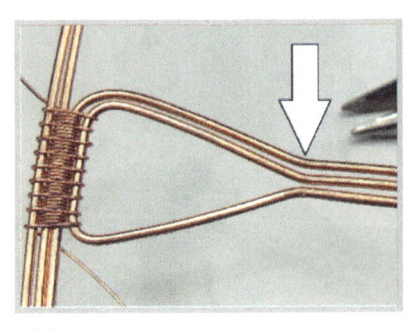

12. At the point where this wire meets with the horizontal part of the previously bent wire, bend it to the right-side direction, to make it horizontal as the other wire ends.

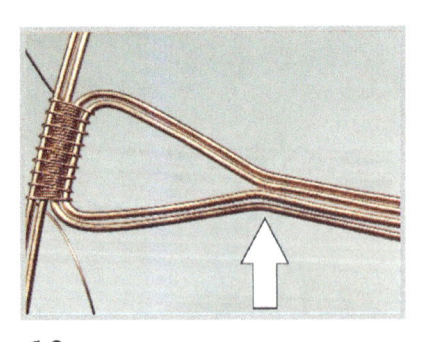

13. Take the lower wire end of this base wire and repeat the same bending steps on the lower side as well, as shown here.

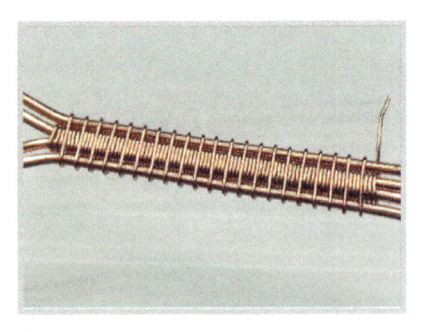

14. Cut a 32 inches (80 cm) long weaving wire of the 26ga (0.4 mm) wire. Repeat the 3-1 central weave around the 4 base wires, until you finish the weaving wire.

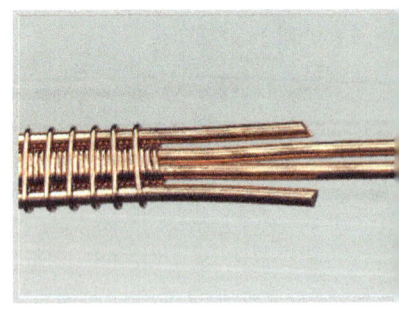

15. Behind the base wire, cut off the short weaving wire end. Leave a 1 cm long end on the outer base wires, cut off the extra ends of them.

16. With the help of the round nose pliers, bend the upper wire end to the left side direction, making a closed loop with it, as shown here.

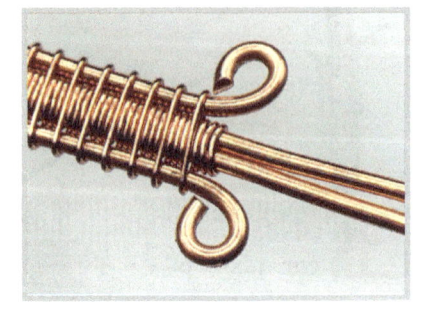

17. Repeat the same step with the lower wire end as well, bending it to the left side direction, making a small, closed loop with it.

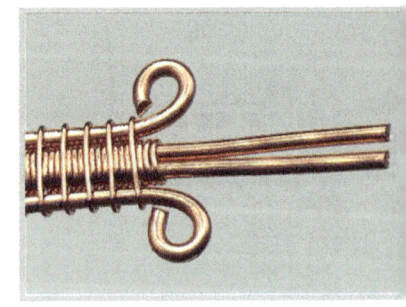

18. Leave a 1,5 cm long end on the 2 inner base wires, cut off the extra ends of them.

TUTORIALS

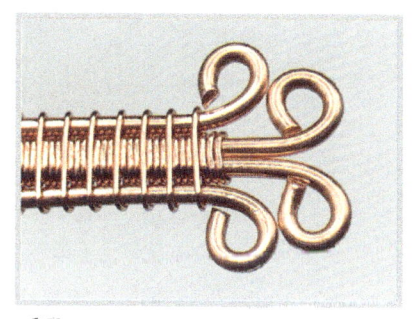

19. Repeat the same bending steps with these 2 inner base wire ends, to make another 2 small loops with them, as shown here.

20. Now we must repeat all these weaving and bending steps on the other side of the bracelet as well, taking another weaving wire of the same length (32 inches / 80 cm long).

21. Position the bead over the central woven part, hiding the whole weave around the center of the base wires.

22. Take both weaving wire ends to the opposite side of the wire structure, through the hole of the bead, as shown here and in the next picture.

23. This is the same step from the top view. Pull the weaving wire ends to the opposite sides until they are wrapped tightly through the hole of the bead.

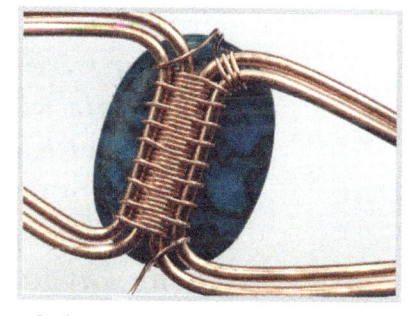

24. On the back, wrap the upper weaving wire end 3 times around the right base wires, as shown on this picture. Cut off the extra weaving wire end on this side. Press it with the chain nose pliers until it is completely closed.

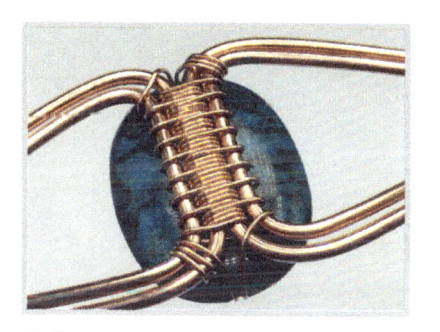

25. Repeat the same steps on the lower side as well. Wrap the weaving wire 3 times around the left base wires, then cut off the extra end of it.

26. Bend your bracelet around a bracelet mandrel or a crystal glass, to make the final shape of it, as shown here. Your beautiful bracelet is ready.

43

Tip:

Once your wire wrapped jewelry is finished, double check if every single wire end has been closed properly. Touch the wire ends with your fingers. If you can feel them, then it is necessary to press the wire ends tighter with the tip of the chain nose pliers. Take a piece of cloth you are not wearing anymore, rub your jewelry tightly with this cloth, to make sure it is safe for wearing and will not damage our clothes.

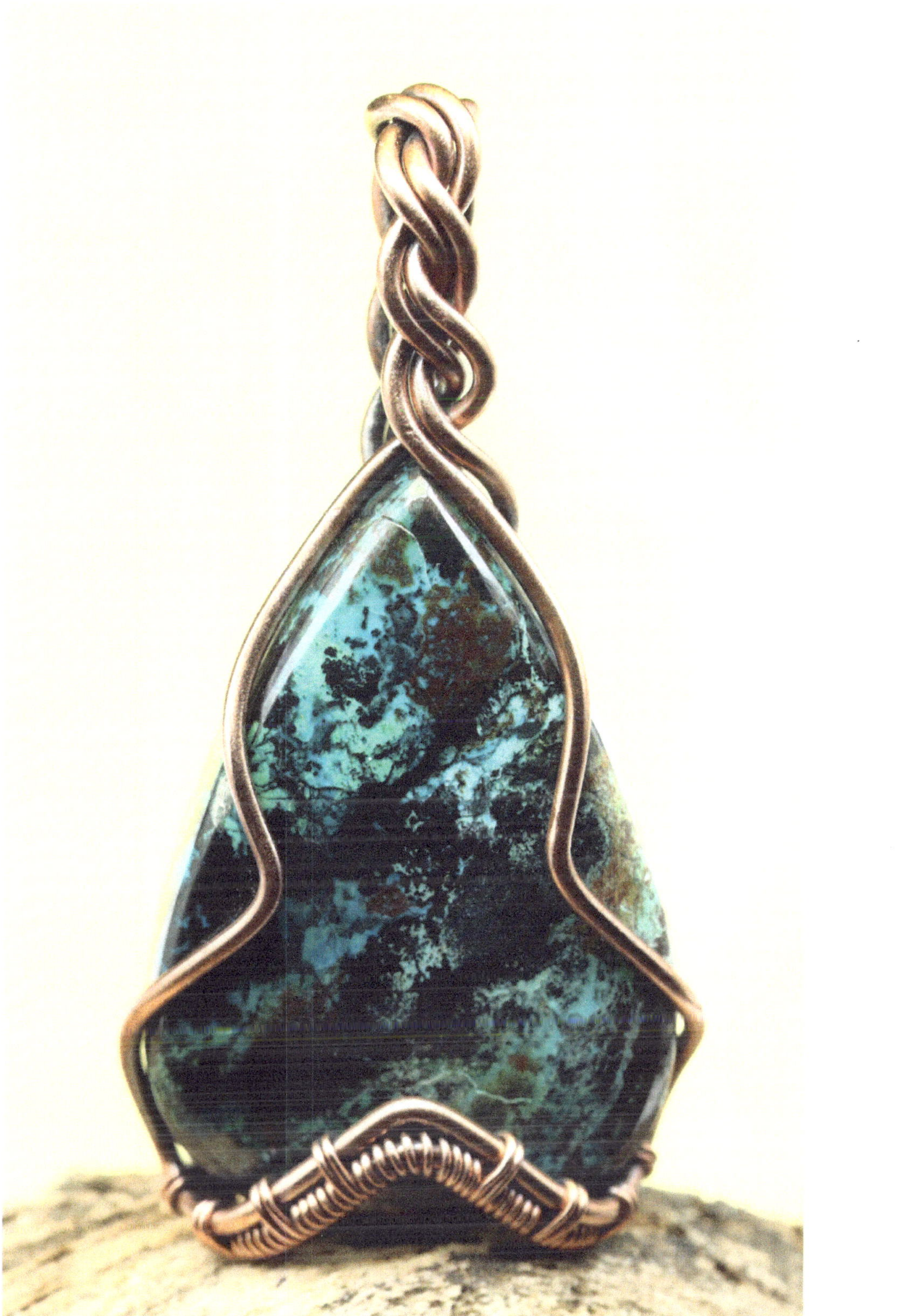

TUTORIALS

Flawless Flame Pendant

In this tutorial, in addition to an already learned wire weaving technique, we will learn a little bit of wire braiding as well. We will need a teardrop shaped cabochon between 25-35 mm big. This one is 30 mm big.
Tools needed: chain (or flat) nose pliers, round nose pliers, wire flush cutter
Wires: -18ga (1 mm) OR 20ga (0.8 mm) wire: 2x 8 inches (20 cm)
       -26ga (0.4 mm) wire: 1x 16 inches (40 cm)

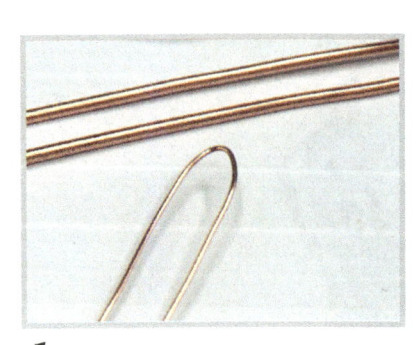

1. Cut 2 base wires of the 18ga (1 mm) wire with the length of 8 inches (20 cm), each. Cut a 16 inches (40 cm) long 26ga (0.4 mm) weaving wire, bend it in half.

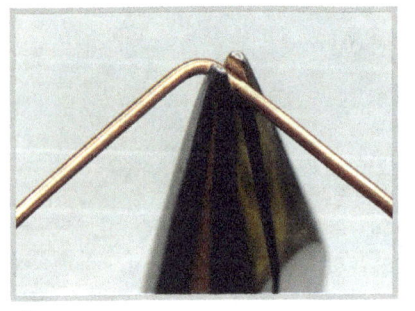

2. Take one of these base wires. Hold the center of it tight within the tip of the chain nose pliers, then bend the left half 90 Degrees downwards, as shown here.

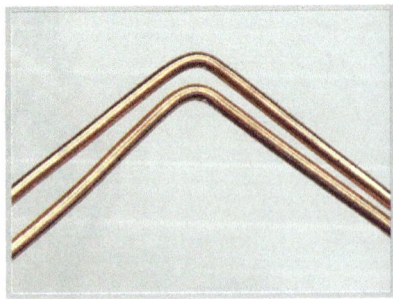

3. Repeat the same step with the other base wire as well, then position these 2 wires close to each other.

46

TUTORIALS

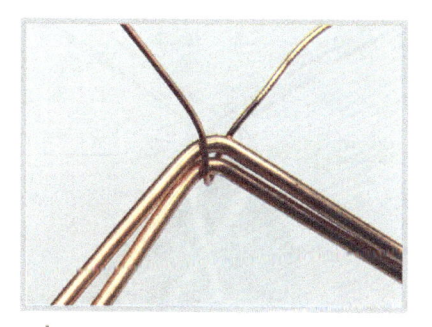

4. Position the bent center of the weaving wire around the bent corner of the base wires, with the weaving wire ends pointed upwards.

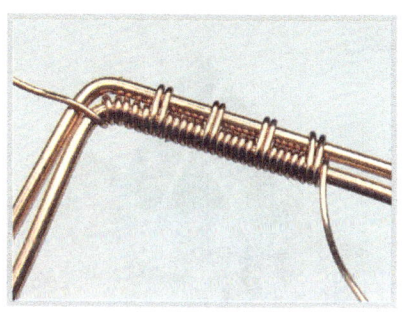

5. With the right end of the weaving wire, make 4 rotations of the 5-2 weave, as tight as possible.

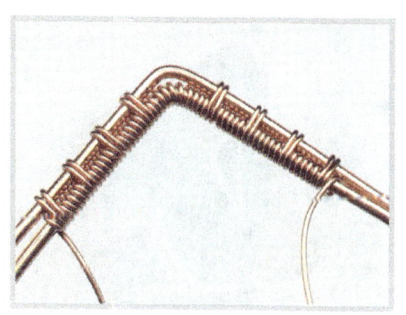

6. Repeat the same steps with the left weaving wire end as well, weaving tightly around the base wires on the left side.

7. Position the woven center of the base wires over the bottom center of the cabochon. The last woven rotations must stay below the stone.

8. Hold the center of the base wires tight between your fingers and the stone, then bend the base wire ends completely backwards below the stone.

9. On the right side, bend the upper base wire to the front, bending it near the right side of the stone, as tight as possible.

10. Now bend this base wire to cross the stone, positioning it slightly below the pointed top of this tone.

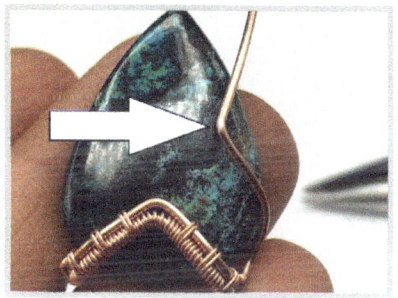

11. At the point shown with the arrow, with the help of the chain nose pliers, bend this wire to the opposite direction, as shown.

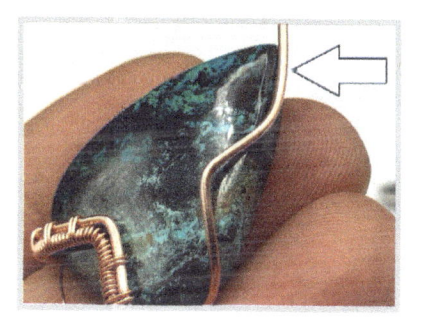

12. Hold the bent part tight between your fingers and the stone, then bend the wire end close to the top right side of the stone (not over the stone, near it).

47

TUTORIALS

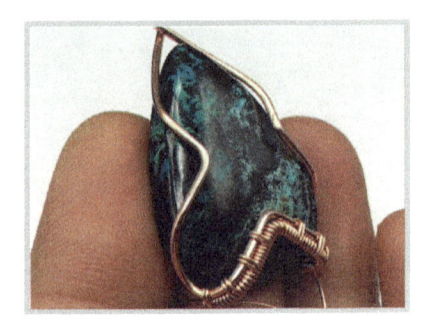

13. *Repeat all these steps on the left side as well, as shown here.*

14. *Switch to the back view. Bend these 2 base wires to cross them over each other below the top of the stone, as shown on this picture.*

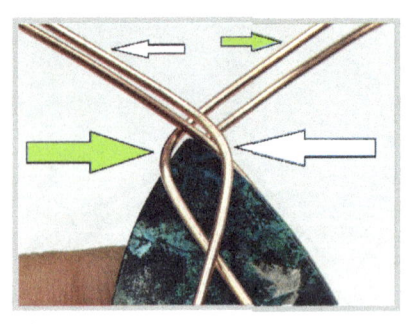

15. *Now we must bend these 2 wires close to the front wires, following their direction, as shown with the arrows. The left wire is bent to the right side behind the other wires (green arrow).*

16. *On the front, position the pendant in horizontal, then straighten the base wires to make them verticals.*

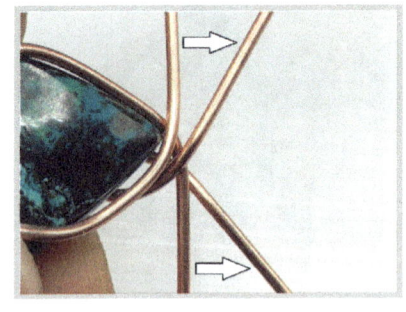

17. *Hold the wires close to the stone. Take the right upper and right lower wire, move them slightly to the right-side direction.*

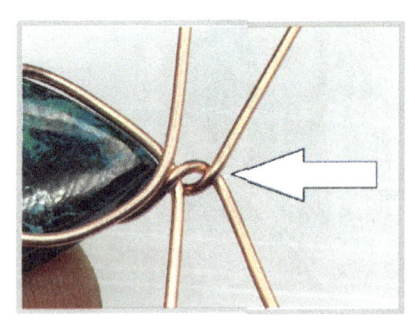

18. *Now make a tight twist with these 2 base wires.*

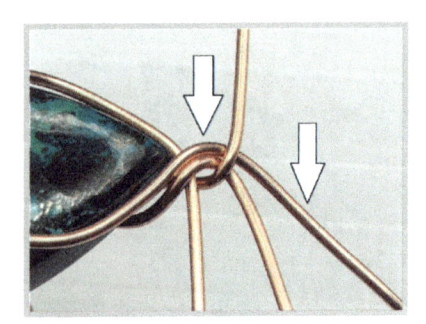

19. *Take the left upper wire, bend it slightly downwards, following the path of the previously twisted wire, and bending it behind the wire pointed upwards.*

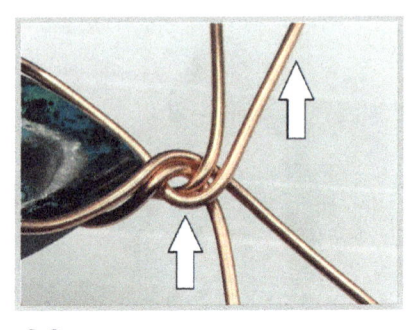

20. *Take the left lower wire, bend it slightly upwards, following the path of the previously twisted wire, and bending it over the wires pointed downwards.*

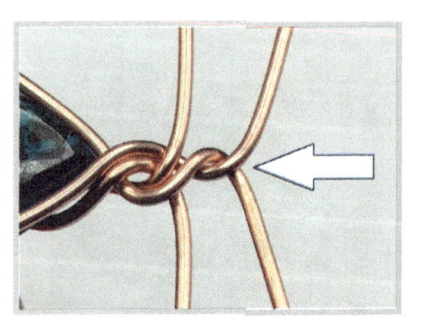

21. *Now twist these 2 recently bent wires once around each other, as shown.*

TUTORIALS

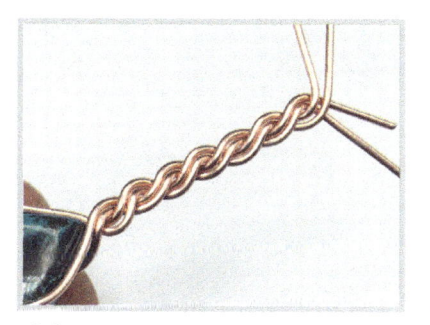

22. *Repeat the same steps until you arrive almost at the end of the base wires. I made 7 rotations of this braid.*

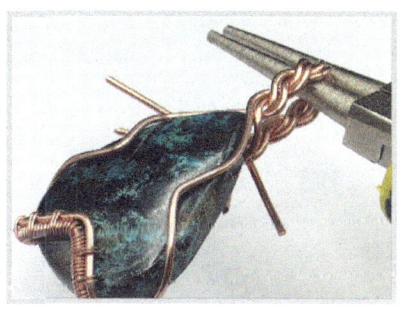

23. *Hold the center of the braid tight within the round nose pliers, then bend the upper half of it backwards, then downwards, to make the bail of the pendant.*

24. *On the back, cut off both weaving wire ends, then press them with the tip of the chain nose pliers, until they are completely closed.*

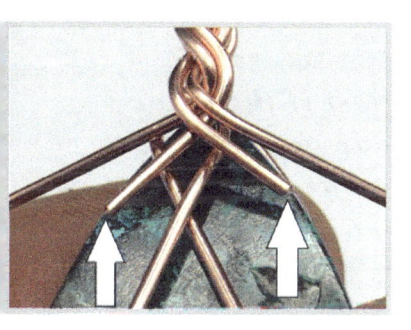

25. *Leave a 0.5 cm long end on these lower base wires shown with the arrows, cut off the extra wire ends.*

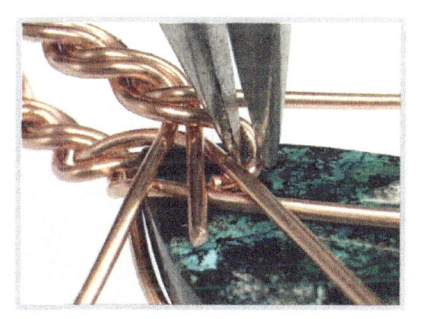

26. *With the tip of the chain nose pliers, bend the right wire end below the crossing base wire over the back of the stone, as shown here.*

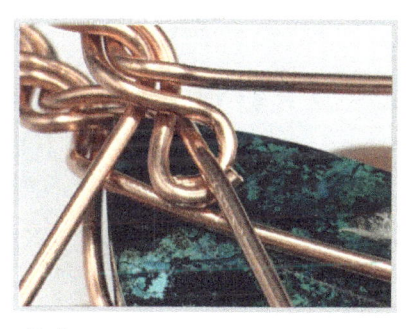

14. *Repeat the same step with the other base wire on the left side as well.*

14. *Leave a 1.5 cm long end on the other 2 base wires, cut off the extra wire ends. With the tip of the round nose pliers, bend the right wire end inwards, making a closed loop with it.*

14. *Repeat the same step with the left wire as well, bending it inwards and making another closed loop with it, as shown.*

Your beautiful cabochon pendant is ready.

49

Tip:

After finishing a cabochon pendant, we can test if the stone has been set tightly, as it is important that our jewelry last for a long time. Hold the bail tightly with your fingers, then move the jewelry very fast in all directions. If the stone has been set firmly, it should not move from the wire structure.

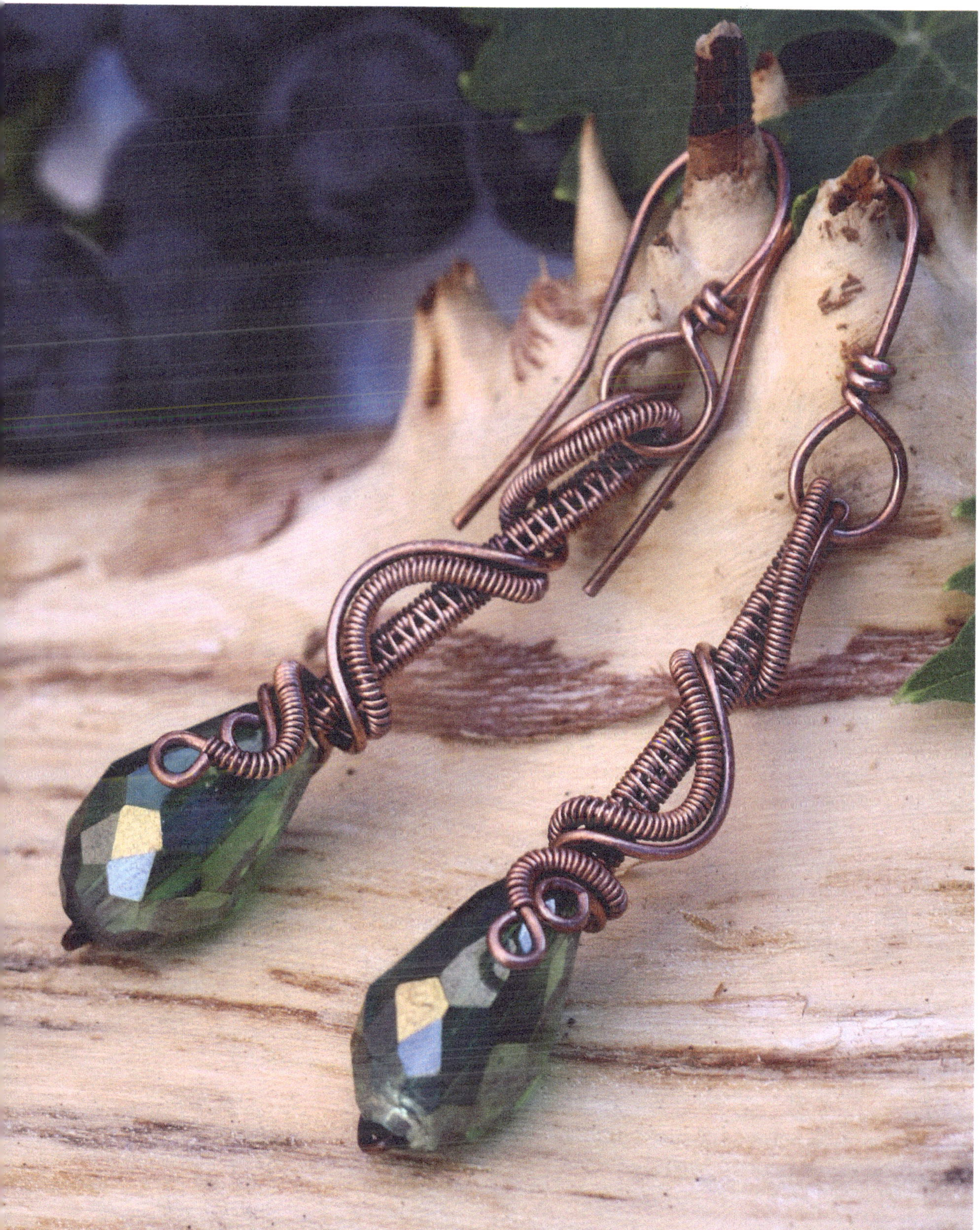

TUTORIALS

Elegant Drop Earrings

In this tutorial we will learn how to create elegant, beaded earrings, with a loop decoration on the beads. We can use any kind of vertically drilled beads between 10-20 mm big.
Tools needed: chain (or flat) nose pliers, round nose plier, wire flush cutter
Wires: -20ga (0.8 mm) wire: 2x 10 inches (25 cm), 2x 3 inches (7.5 cm)
        -28ga (0.3 mm) wire: 2x 40 inches (100 cm)

1. Materials and tools for this project are shown on this picture. The crystal beads I chose to use for these earrings are 15 mm tall.

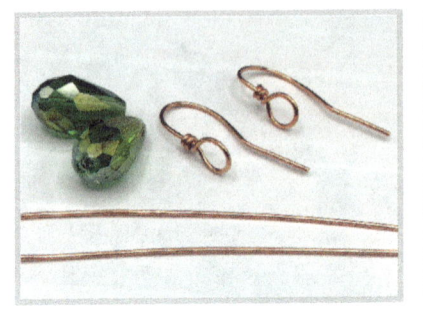

2. First we will make the ear wires as we learned in the techniques section. For the earrings cut 2 base wires of the 20ga (0.8 mm) wire, with the length of 10 inches (25 cm), each.

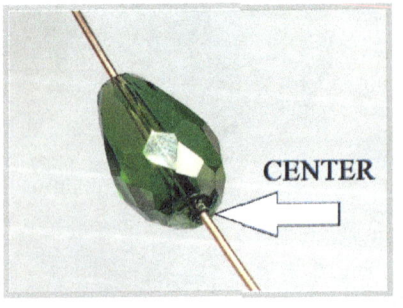

3. Take one of these base wires, add your bead to the center of this wire, having the center at the bottom of the bead, as shown.

52

TUTORIALS

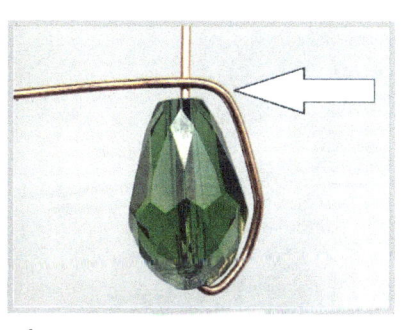

4. Bend the lower half of the base wire all around the right side of the bead, exactly in the same way as shown here.

5. Close to the hole of the bead at the top, hold the bent base wire tight within the tip of the chain nose pliers, then bend it completely upwards.

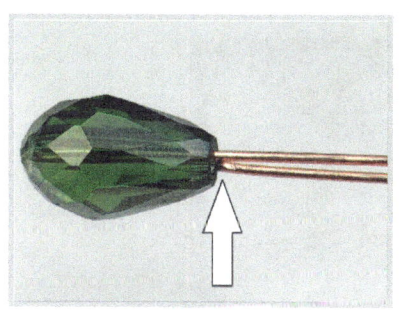

6. Position the wire ends horizontally in a way that both are on the front. The bent wire must remain hidden behind the bead and positioned below the other base wire end on the front.

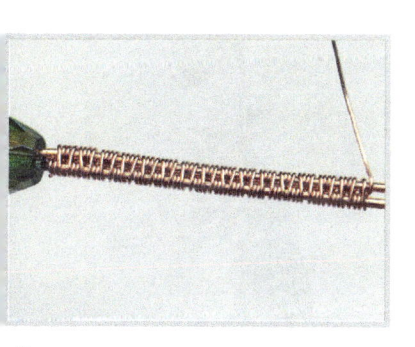

7. Take a 40 inches (100 cm) long weaving wire of the 28ga (0.3 mm) wire. Make a 2.5 cm long woven section of the 2-1 zig zag weave around the base wires.

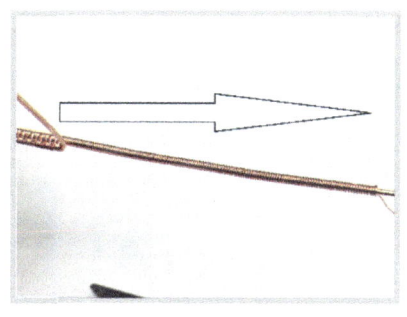

8. Now bend the lower base wire completely toward yourself and coil the weaving wire 140 times around the upper base wire, very tightly.

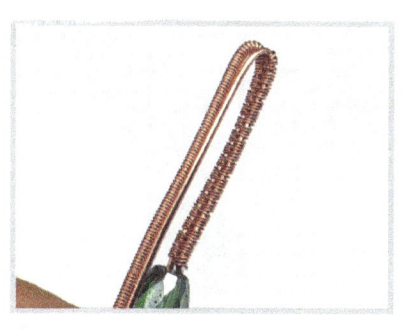

9. At the point where the zig zag weave ends, bend both base wires to the front, then bend them downwards over the bead, as shown here.

10. Add the ear wire to the wire structure, positioning it to the top, as shown here.

11. Close to the top of the wire structure, bend both base wires slightly to the right-side direction, as shown here.

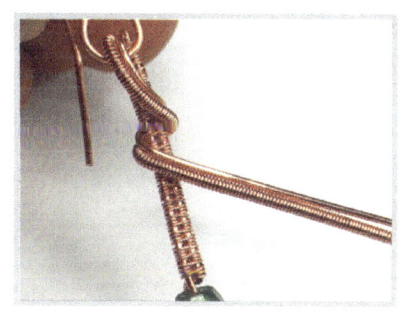

12. Hold the wires at the top tight between your fingers, then wrap both wires together around the zig zag weave, as shown.

53

TUTORIALS

13. Bend these 2 wires together, to make a half circle shape over the zig zag weave, as shown with the arrow. Now the wires are pointed to the left-side direction.

14. Hold the curved part of the wires tight between your fingers, then wrap these wires around the bottom of the zig zag weave, over the top of the bead.

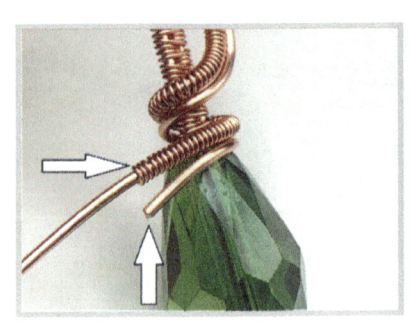

15. We must have a 0.5 cm long coile part on the front, otherwise make a fe more coils, then cut off the weaving wir end. Leave a 0.5 cm long end on the lowe base wire, on the front.

16. With the tip of the round nose pliers, bend the lower wire end to the right-side direction, making a small, closed loop with it, as shown.

17. Bend the coiled base wire all around the left side of this small loop.

18. Leave a 0.5 cm long end on this base wire (counting from the end of the coiled part), cut off the extra wire end.

19. With the tip of the round nose pliers, bend the short wire end to the left-side direction, making a small, closed loop with it, as shown.

20. One earring is ready. Now we will make the second one, symmetrical to this one. For the second earring we will repeat the same steps between 3-7.

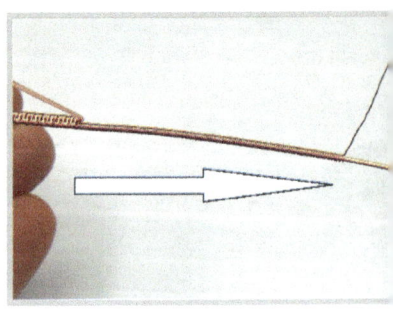

21. Now bend the upper base wire completely toward yourself and coil the weaving wire 140 times around the lower base wire, very tightly.

TUTORIALS

22. At the point where the zig zag weave ends, bend both base wires to the front, then bend them downwards over the bead, as shown here. Add the ear wire to the wire structure.

23. Close to the top of the wire structure, bend both base wires slightly to the left-side direction, as shown here.

24. Hold the wires at the top, tight between your fingers, then wrap both wires together around the zig zag weave, as shown.

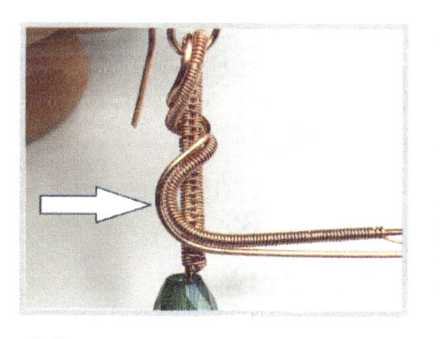

25. Bend these 2 wires together, to make a half circle shape over the zig zag weave, as shown with the arrow. Now the wires are pointed to the right-side direction.

26. Hold the curved part of the wires tight between your fingers, then wrap these wires around the bottom of the zig zag weave, over the top of the bead.

27. Leave a 0.5 cm end on the lower base wire on the front, cut off the extra end of it, then bend it into a closed loop. Cut off the extra weaving wire end.

28. Bend the other base wire around the small loop. Leave a 0.5 cm end on this wire (counting from the end of the coiled part), cut off the extra wire end.

29. With the tip of the round nose pliers, bend the short wire end to the right-side direction, making a small, closed loop with it, as shown.

Your beautiful earrings are ready.

55

Tip:

To photoshoot our jewelry, we must make sure that we have good lightning. Copper jewelry shines beautifully in an outdoor environment. In this case we must choose the shadow to create a beautiful picture of our jewelry. We can also opt for a lightbox to create amazing pictures indoors, anytime we wish.

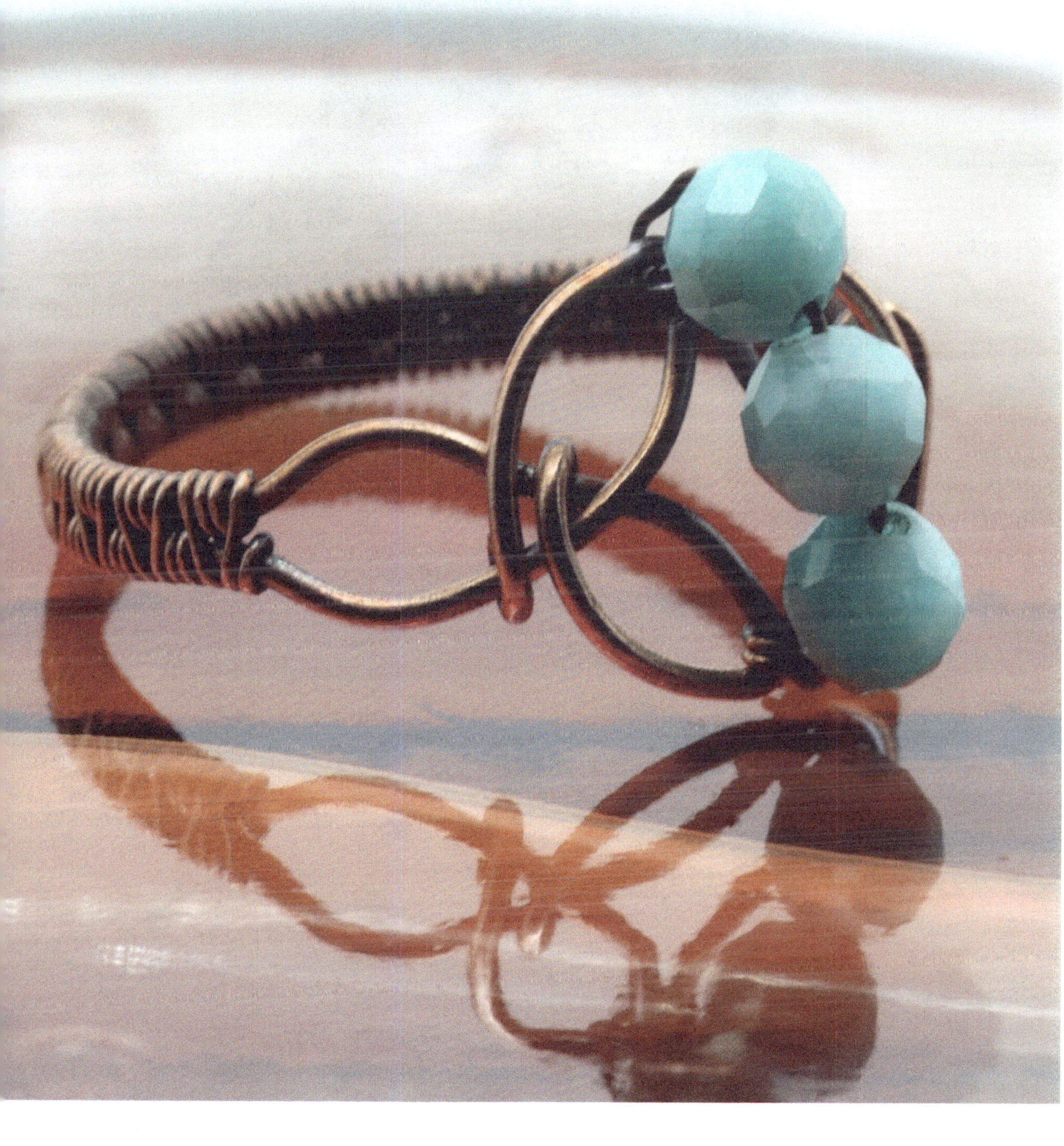

TUTORIALS

Celtic Beaded Ring

In this tutorial we will learn how to wire wrap a Celtic flower shape, with the combination of a wire weaving technique shown before. We will need to take 3 beads of maximum 4 mm big each.
Tools needed: chain (or flat) nose pliers, ring mandrel (or wooden dowel), wire flush cutter
Wires: -20ga (0.8 mm) wire: 2x 6 inches (15 cm)
         -26ga (0.4 mm) wire: 1x 28 inches (70 cm), 1x 4 inches (10 cm)

1. Take any wire, wrap it once around the ring mandrel, over the ring size you wish to make. Cut off the extra wire end. This wire measures the length of the ring circumference.

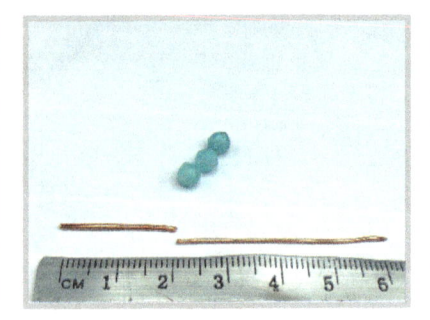

2. Straighten this wire, then cut off a 2 cm length from the initial part of it, as shown here. This 2 cm length will be covered with the flower shape later.

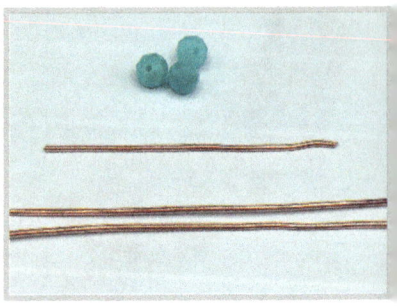

3. Cut 2 base wires of the 20ga (0.8 mm) wire, with the length of 6 inches (15 cm), each.

58

TUTORIALS

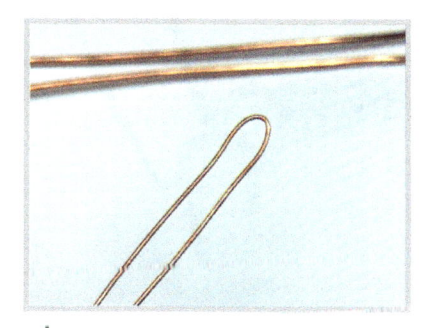

4. Cut a 28 inches (70 cm) long weaving wire of the 26ga (0.4 mm) wire. Bend it in half, as shown here.

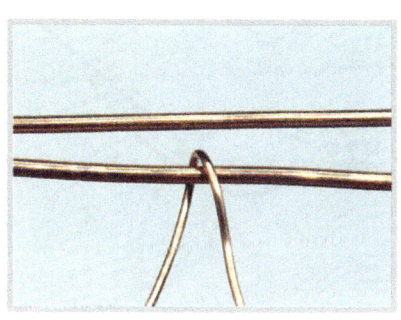

5. Hold both base wires together, making sure that the ends of them are aligned. Position the bent center of the weaving wire around the center of the lower base wire.

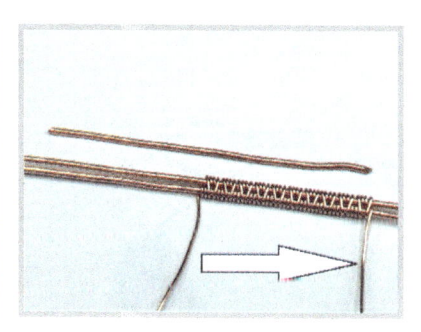

6. With the right end of the weaving wire we must follow the compressed 2-1 zigzag weave around these 2 base wires, until the length of the woven part covers half the length of the short wire.

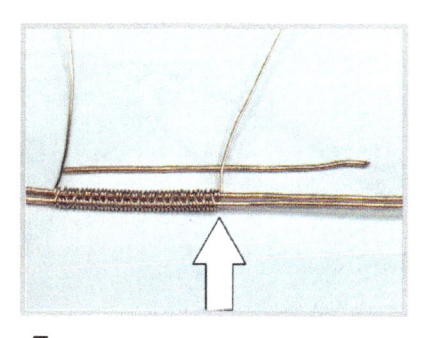

7. Turn the wires from the right side to the left side, clockwise, so the recently made woven part is positioned on the left side now.

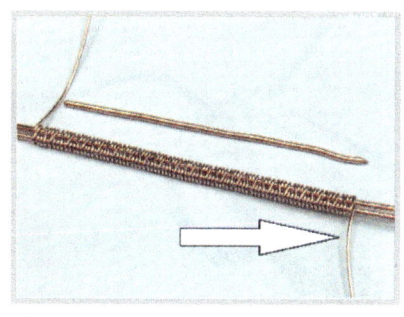

8. With this other weaving wire end repeat the same weaving steps until the whole woven part has the same length as the short wire.

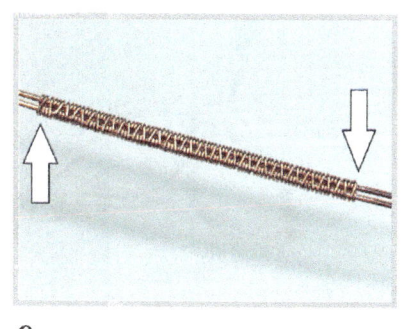

9. On both ends of the woven part, cut off the extra weaving wire ends behind the base wires, then press them with the tip of the chain nose pliers, to close them.

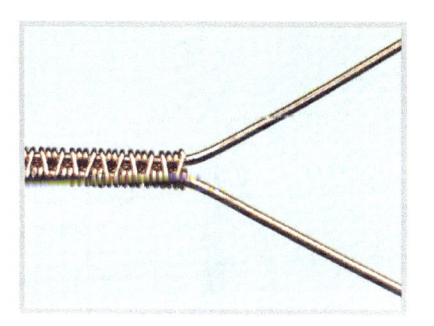

10. We will make the Celtic flower on the right side. Separate the 2 base wires, as shown here.

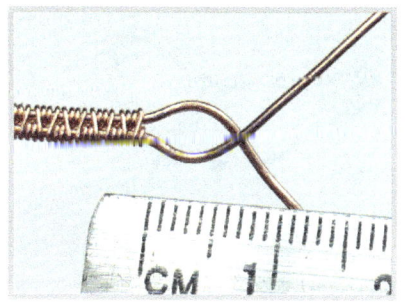

11. Now bend them to the opposite directions, making a small curve with them, and crossing the lower wire over the upper one at a 0.5 cm distance from the end of the weave.

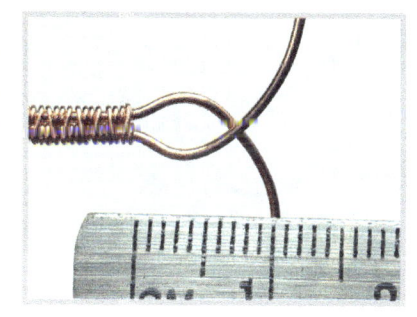

12. Bend both wire ends to make them vertical, continuing the curve we made with them before. The vertical part of the wires must be at a 1 cm distance from the end of the woven part.

59

TUTORIALS

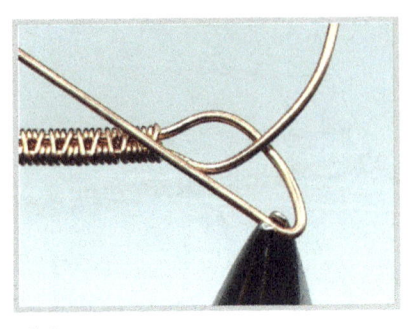

13. From the crossing point of the wires, measure 0.5 cm on the lower wire. At this point hold it tight within the tip of the chain nose pliers and bend it to the opposite direction.

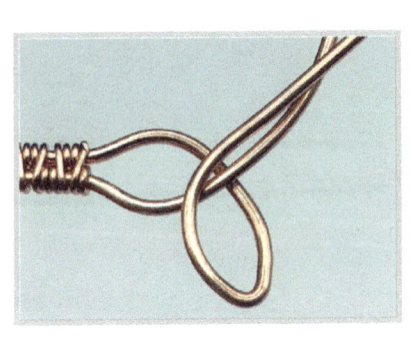

14. Continue to bend the wire end, making a leaf shape with it and positioning it close to the upper base wire, as shown here.

15. Hold this leaf shape tight within your fingers then bend the wire end backwards (slightly downwards), over the crossing point of the base wires.

16. Switch to the back view. Leave a very short end on this wire, cut off the extra end of it.

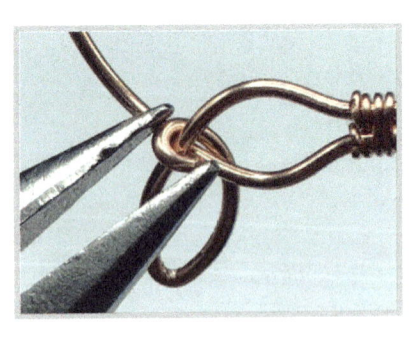

17. With the tip of the chain nose pliers, press the short wire end behind the other wire, until it is completely closed.

18. Switch to the front view. Measure 0.5 cm on the upper wire as well, then bend it to the opposite direction, as shown here.

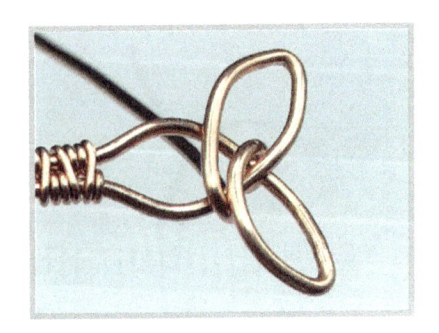

19. Hold this leaf shape tight within your fingers then bend the wire end backwards, slightly upwards, as shown.

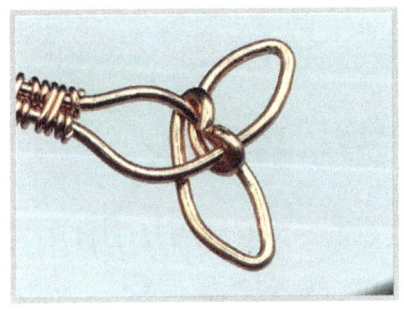

20. As we did with the other wire end, on the back, cut off the extra end of this wire as well, then press it with the tip of the chain nose pliers until it is completely closed.

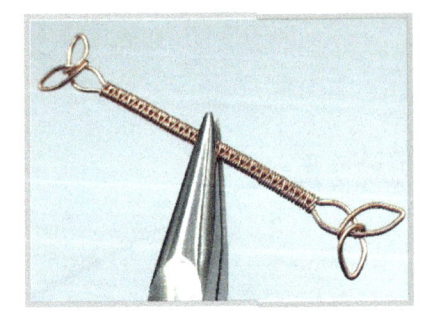

21. Turn the wire structure from the right to the left, clockwise, then repeat the same bending steps with these other 2 wire ends as well, to make another Celtic flower of the same size.

60

TUTORIALS

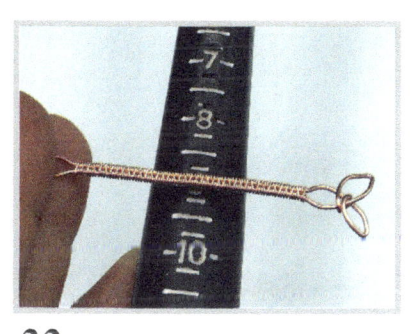

22. Position the center of the woven part over the ring mandrel (or wooden dowel), as shown.

23. Bend both sides of the wire structure all around the mandrel, until the 2 flowers meet on the other side of it

24. Separate the ring from the mandrel. Cut a 4 inches (10 cm) long 26ga (0.4 mm) weaving wire. Wrap the initial end of it 2 times around the top of the 2 flowers, to connect them.

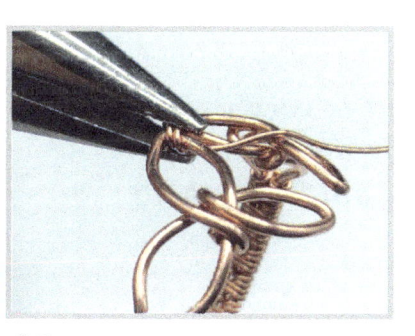

25. Behind the base wires, cut off the short extra wire end, then press it with the tip of the chain nose pliers, until it is completely closed.

26. Position the weaving wire above the woven part at the top of the flowers. Add 3 beads to this weaving wire

27. Hold these 3 beads together, then bend them slowly over the center of the ring, positioning them in between the 2 Celtic flowers.

28. Take the weaving wire to the front through the lower part of the left flower, as shown here.

14. Wrap the weaving wire 2 times around the lower side of the 2 flowers, to connect them. Cut off the extra wire end, then press it with the tip of the pliers to close it completely.

Your beautiful Celtic flower ring is ready.

TIP: You can add 1 larger bead to the center and 2 smaller beads to the sides, to create another effect.

61

Tip:

Every time we create a wire wrapped ring, it is very useful if we insert the ring into the mandrel upside down as well, to make sure that both sides of the ring are uniformly bent around the mandrel.

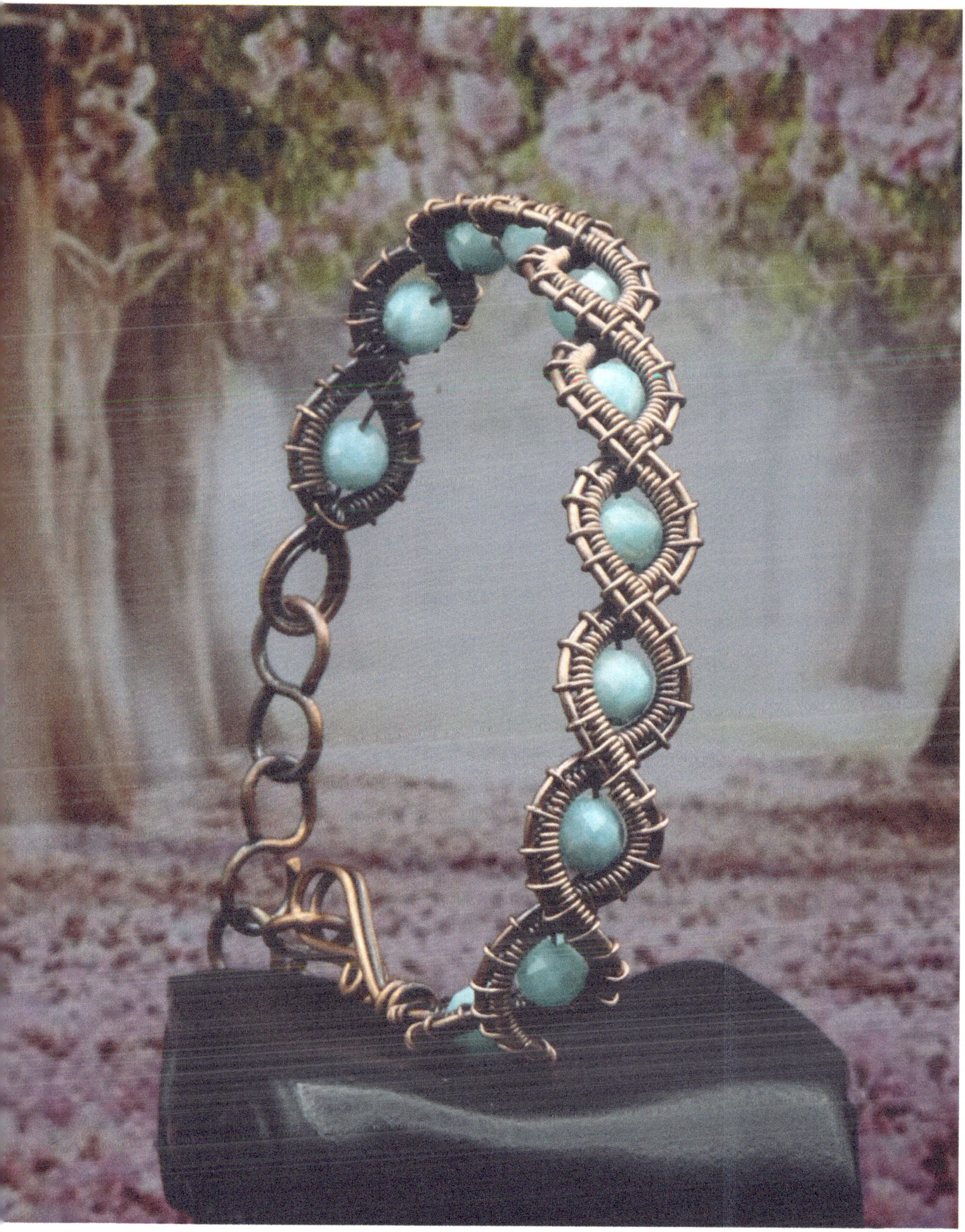

TUTORIALS

Beaded Bracelet

Archeologists think that early humans may have created and worn beaded bracelets up 75.000 years ago, expressing their individuality and title. Native American Indians have worn beaded bracelets dating back to prehistoric times. They used natural metals, animal bones, and stones like turquoise and shells.
With the passage of time, handmade beaded jewelry started to become a status symbol.
Today we can add many types of beads to our jewelry, the most common are the glass, porcelain, shell, clay, metal, gemstones and even wood beads.
In this tutorial we will learn how to create a beautiful, beaded bracelet. Measurements are for a small bracelet, in case you wish to create a bigger one, please use longer base and weaving wires.
Tools needed: chain (or flat) nose pliers, round nose pliers, wire cutter
Wires: -20ga (0.8 mm): 2x 16 inches (40 cm)
-26ga (0.4 mm) wire: 1x 10 inches (25 cm), 1x 100 inches (250 cm)
-round shaped beads of 4 mm big each, approximately 11 pieces or more

TUTORIALS

1. *Materials and tools for this project are shown on this picture. These beads are 4 mm natural gemstone beads.*

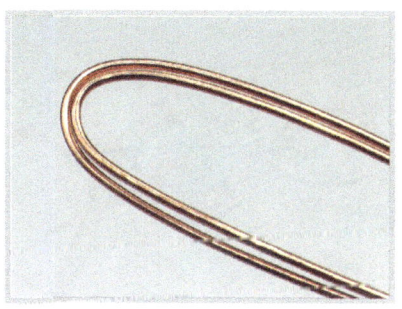

2. *Cut 2 base wires of the 20ga (0.8 mm) wire, with the length of 16 inches (40 cm), each. Hold them together then bend them in half, as shown here.*

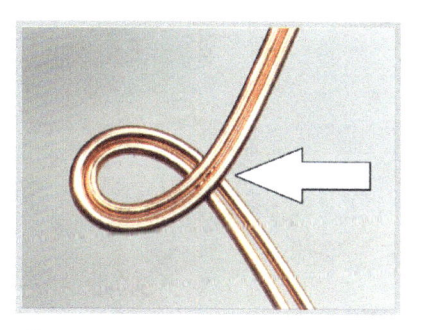

3. *Continue to bend the lower wire ends over the upper ones until you make a small loop with the center of the base wires, approximately 1 cm big.*

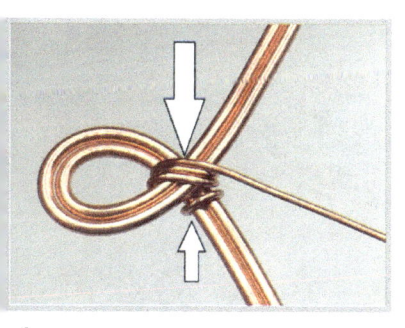

4. *Take a 10 inches (25 cm) long 26ga (0.4 mm) weaving wire. Wrap the initial end of it 3 times around the crossing base wires, then close the end if it over the lower wires.*

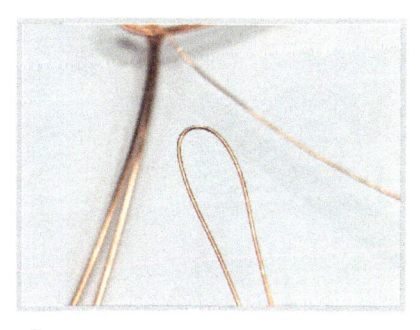

5. *Now cut a 100 inches (250 cm) long weaving wire, bend it in half, as shown here.*

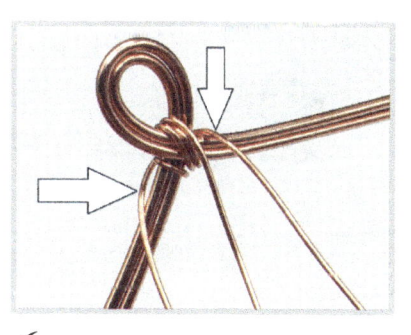

6. *Position the bent center of this long weaving wire around the bottom of the loop, one wire end on the top and the other one on the lower side.*

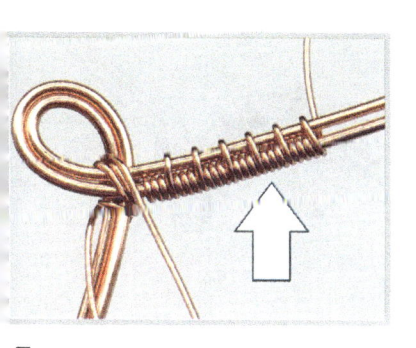

7. *With the upper longer weaving wire end, make 6 rotations of the 3-1 weave around the upper base wires, as tight as you can.*

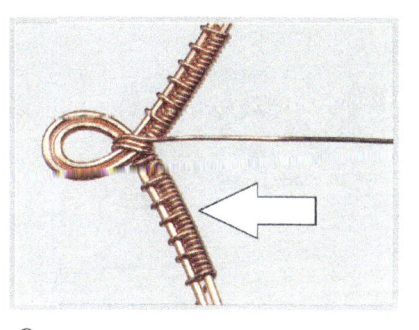

8. *With the lower longer weaving wire end, make 6 rotations of the 3-1 weave around the lower base wires.*

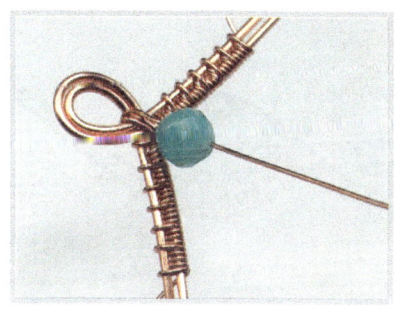

9. *Add a bead to the shorter weaving wire. We will use this weaving wire for the beading only. Position the bead close to the loop of the base wires.*

65

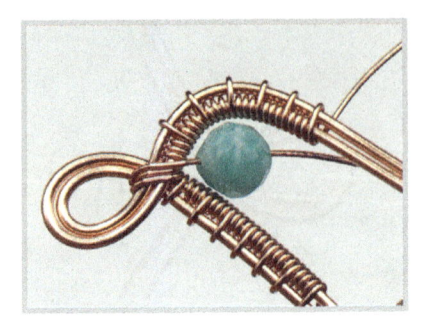

TUTORIALS

10. Bend the upper woven part all around the upper side of the bead, as shown on this picture.

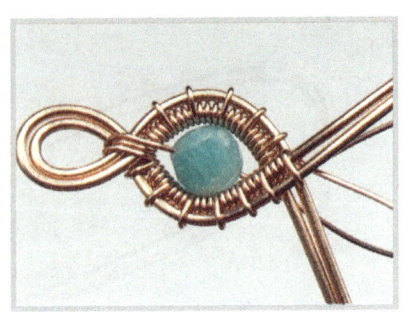

11. Now bend the lower woven part all around the lower side of the bead, bending these wire ends upwards over the other base wire ends which are pointed downwards.

12. Take the beading weaving wire, wrap it once around the right base wire of the 2 wires which are pointed downwards, as shown here.

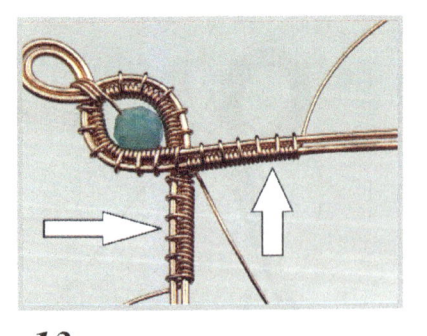

13. Keep the 2 longer weaving wires in their position. With the upper one, make 6 rotations of the 3-1 weave around the upper wire ends, and vice versa.

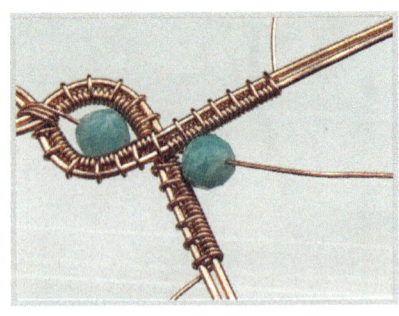

14. Once we have another woven part on the upper and lower sides, add another bead to the central weaving wire, positioning it close to the woven base wires.

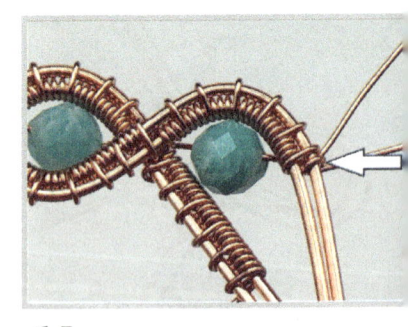

15. Bend the upper woven base wires all around the upper side of the bead, then wrap the beaded weaving wire once around the right base wire end.

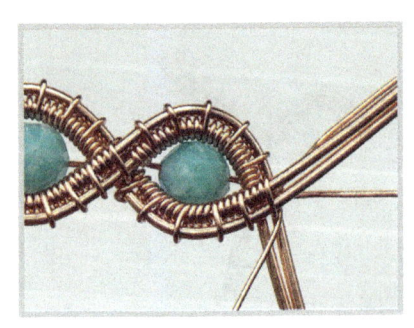

16. Now bend the lower woven part all around the lower side of the bead, bending these wire ends upwards over the other base wire ends which are pointed downwards.

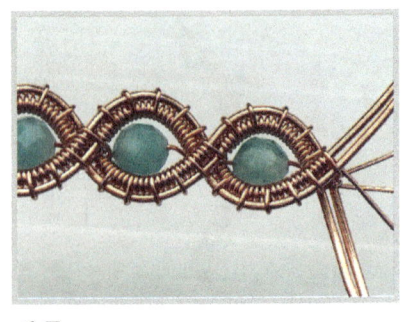

17. Repeat the same step until you add 11 beads approximately and you arrive close to the end of the weaving wires, on the upper and on the lower sides.

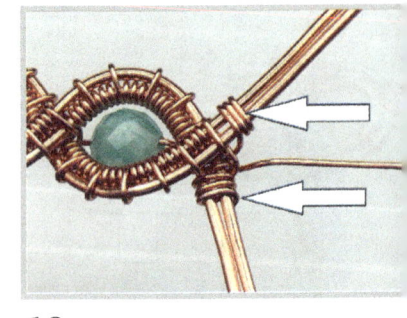

18. Wrap both weaving wires 3 time around the base wires, as shown, then c off the extra ends of them. Press th weaving wire ends with the chain nos pliers, to close them completely.

66

TUTORIALS

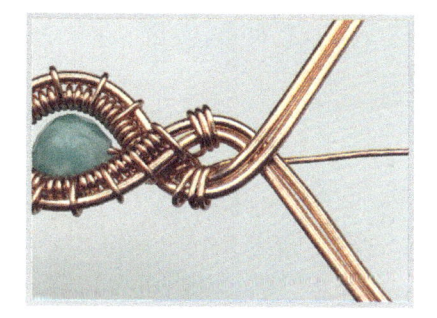

19. Repeat the same bending steps with the base wires as we did with the woven parts before, bending the lower wire ends upwards, over the wires pointed downwards.

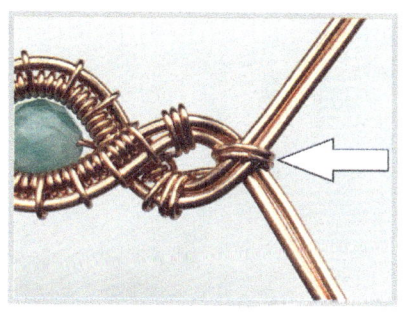

20. Wrap the central weaving wire 2 times around the crossing point of the base wires, then cut off the extra end of it.

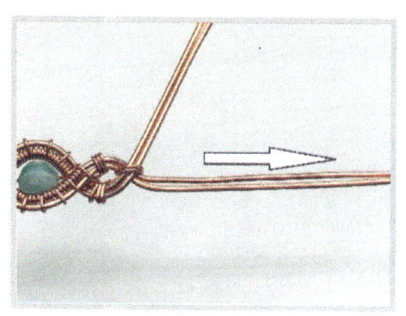

21. Now bend the lower wires slightly upwards, to make them horizontals, as shown here.

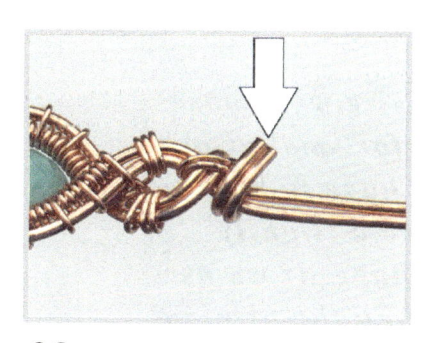

22. Wrap the upper base wire ends once around the horizontal wires, then cut off the extra ends of them, leaving very short wire ends, as shown.

23. Press the short wire ends backwards with the tip of the chain nose pliers, until they are completely closed.

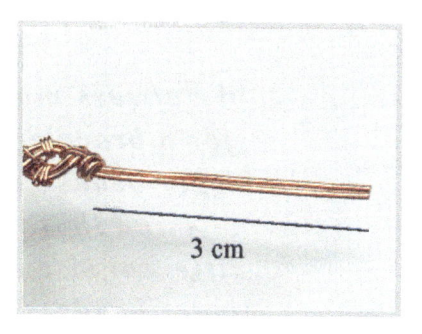

24. Leave a 3 cm long part on these 2 horizontal base wires, cut off the extra ends of them.

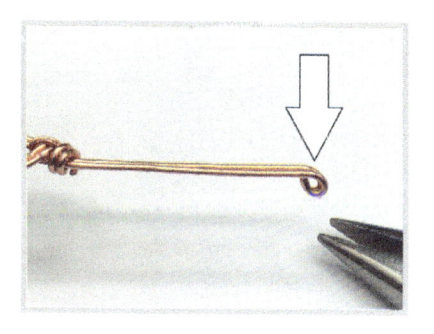

25. With the tip of the chain nose pliers, bend the wire ends to the left side direction, making a very small, closed loop with them, as shown here.

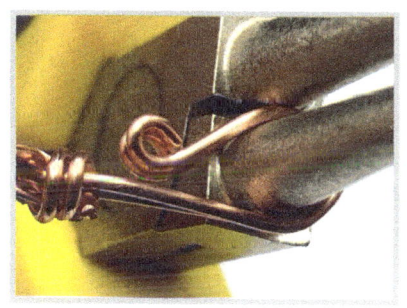

26. Hold the center of these wires tight within the bottom of the round nose pliers, then bend the right end of them to the left side, making a hook with the wire ends.

27. Bend your bracelet around a bracelet mandrel or a crystal glass, then add a piece of chain you like to the other end, with links large enough to pass the hook through to secure the bracelet.

67

Tip:

We always must pay attention to the bead size we choose for a bracelet project. If we decide to opt for smaller or bigger beads than the tutorial requires, we have to keep in mind that the finished bracelet will have a slightly different size once we bend it to its final shape. If we use bigger beads, the bracelet will be smaller than the original one, as the beads will occupy more space between the wire structure and the arm. It is good to keep this in mind.

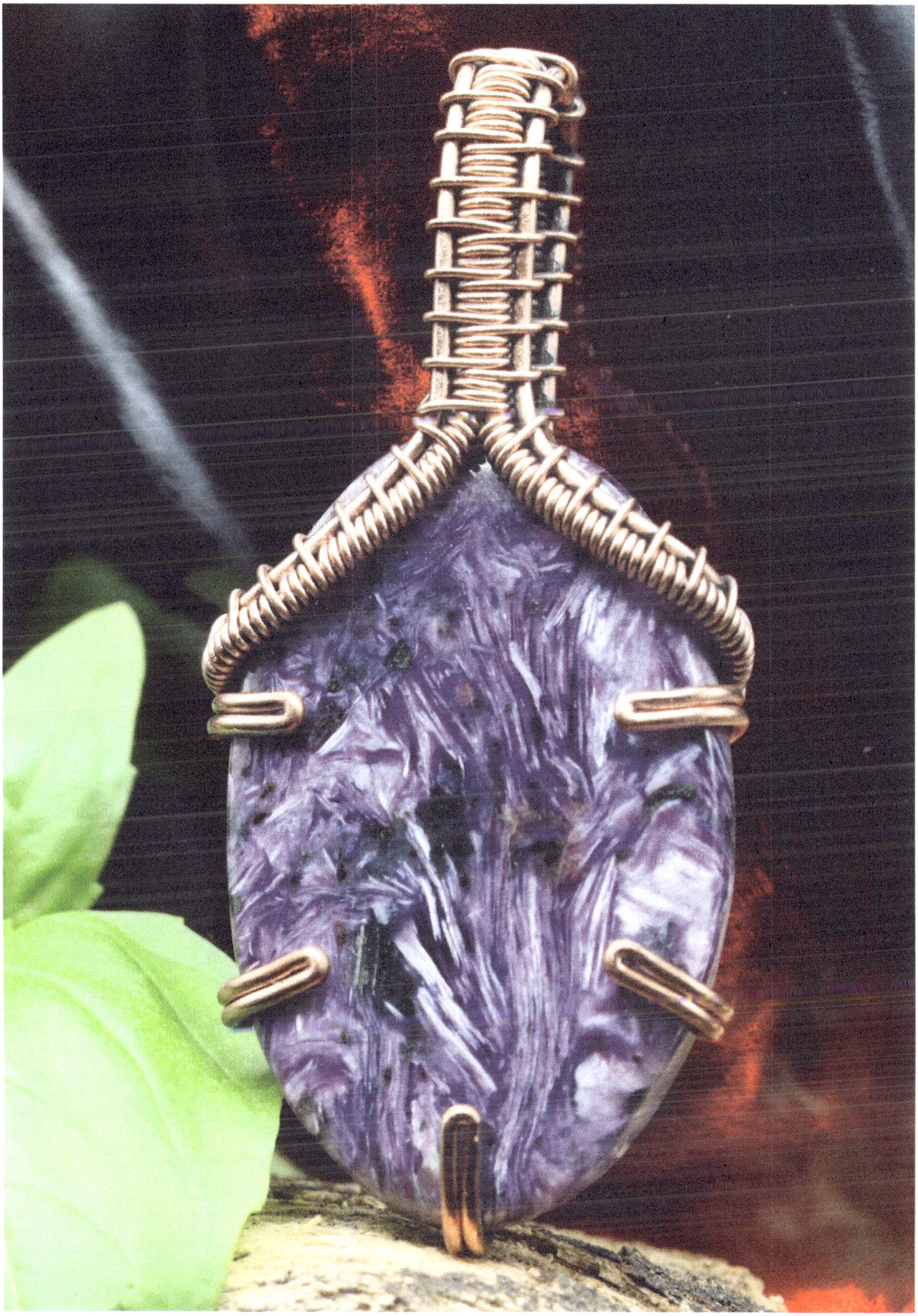

TUTORIALS

Prong Setting Pendant

Prong settings are often incorporated in wire wrapped jewelry as they are elegant, decorative, and the stone is set securely. For this design we can use a 30 mm tall, oval or teardrop shaped cabochon.
Tools needed: chain (or flat) nose pliers, round nose pliers, wire flush cutter
Wires: - 20ga (0.8 mm) wire: 1x 10 inches (25 cm), 1x 14 inches (35 cm)
*   -26ga (0.4 mm) wire: 1x 40 inches (100 cm), 1x 24 inches (60 cm)*

1. *Materials and tools for this project are shown on this picture. The stone I will use is a 30 mm tall oval shaped cabochon.*

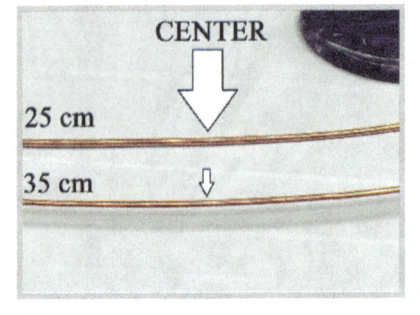

2. *Cut one 10 inches (25 cm) long and a 14 inches (35 cm) long base wire of the 20ga (0.8 mm) wire. Position the longer wire below the shorter one, making sure that the center of them is aligned.*

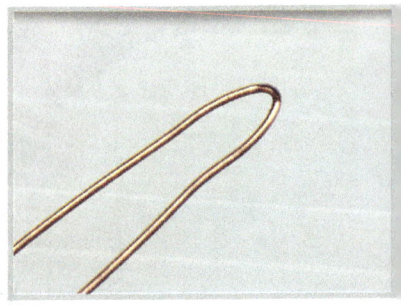

3. *Take a 40 inches (100 cm) long weaving wire of the 26ga (0.4 mm) wire. Bend it in half as shown here.*

70

TUTORIALS

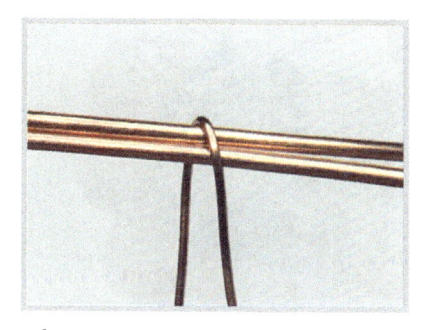

4. *Position the bent center of the weaving wire around the center of these base wires.*

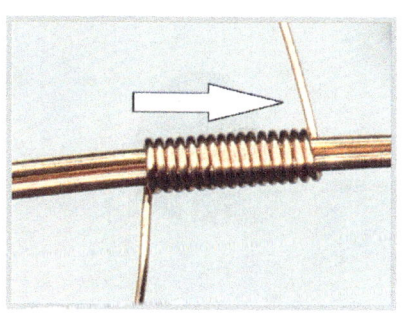

5. *Take the front end of the weaving wire, wrap it 15 times around both base wires, as tight as possible.*

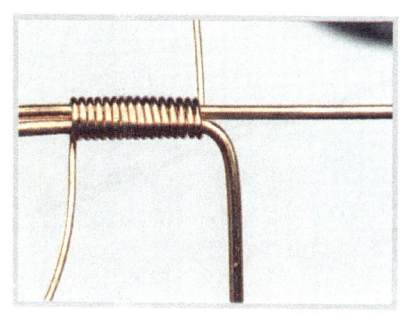

6. *At the point where the woven part ends, bend the lower (longer) base wire end 90 Degrees downwards.*

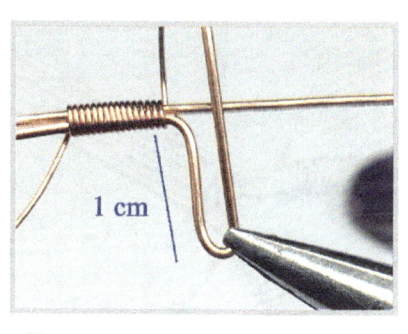

7. *Measure 1 cm length on this base wire, at this point hold it tight within the tip of the chain nose pliers and bend it completely upwards, as shown.*

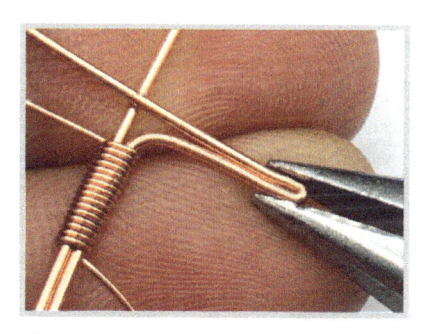

8. *With the tip of the chain nose pliers, press the bent part of the wire until it is completely closed.*

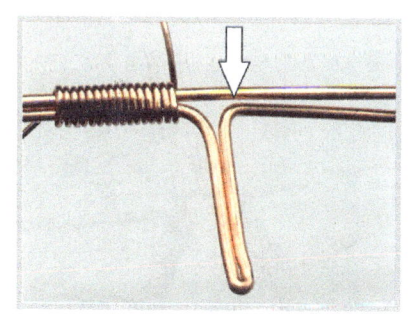

9. *Where the bent wire meets with the upper base wire, hold it tight within the chain pliers and bend it to the right-side direction. 1 prong is ready.*

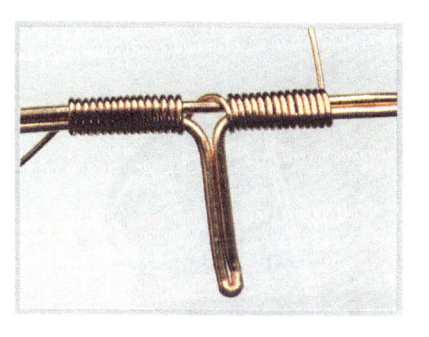

10. *Now again, on the right side of the prong, wrap the weaving wire 15 times around both base wires, as tight as possible.*

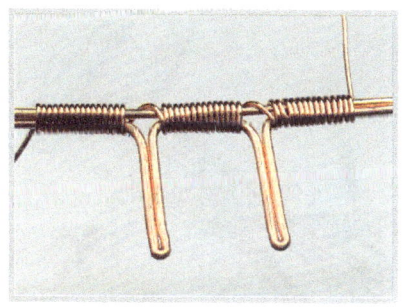

11. *Repeat the same steps one more time, to make a second prong on the right side of the base wires, then wrap the weaving wire 15 times around both base wires.*

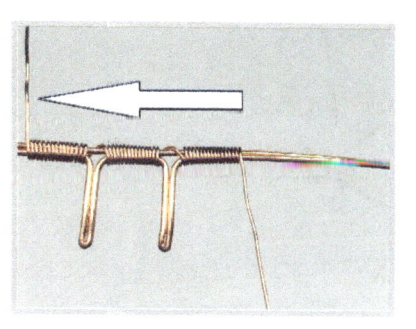

12. *Turn the wire structure from the right side to the left side, upside down, so the recently made prongs are on the left side.*

71

TUTORIALS

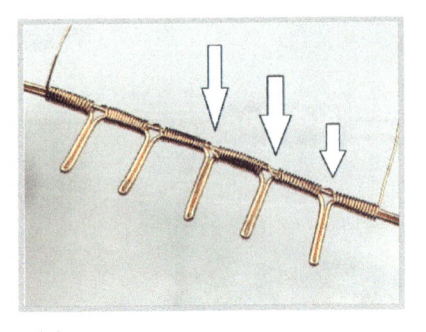

13. Now we must make 3 prongs on this other side of the base wires, following the same bending and weaving steps as we did on the other side before.

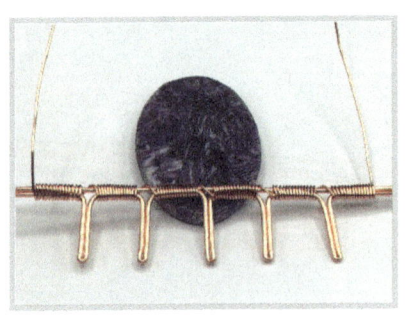

14. Position the central prong over the bottom center of the cabochon, as shown here. The woven base wires must stay over the inner side of the stone.

15. Bend the woven base wires with the prongs all over the inner side of the stone, until the wire ends cross over each other at the top center of the stone (near the ends of the woven

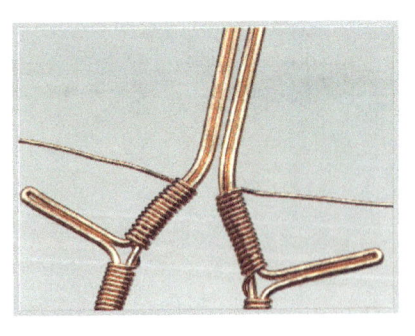

16. At this point, where the woven parts end, bend all 4 base wire ends upwards, as shown here.

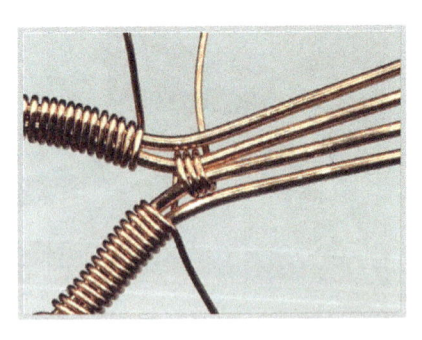

17. Cut a 24 inches (60 cm) long weaving wire of the 26ga (0.4 mm) wire. Wrap the initial end of it 3 times around the 2 inner base wires.

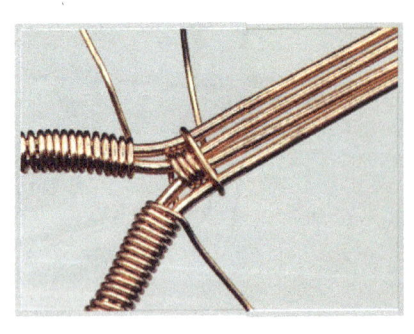

18. Now wrap this weaving wire once around all the 4 base wires. This is another way to use the 3-1 central weave.

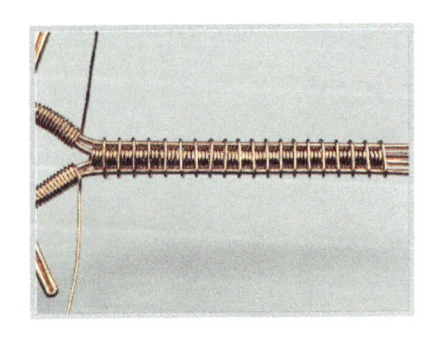

19. Make 20 rotations of the 3-1 central weave, then cut off the extra weaving wire end. Make sure that the woven part is compressed, otherwise push it to the left side until it is.

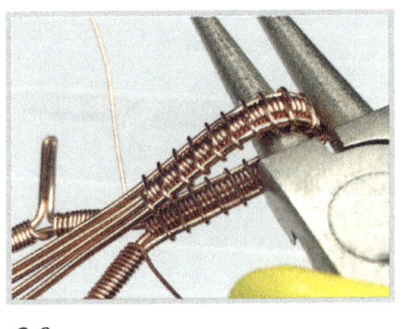

20. Hold the center of the woven part tight within the bottom center of the round nose pliers, then bend the upper half to the front, then downwards, to create the bail of the pendant.

21. Position your cabochon over the center of the wire structure, making sure that each prong has the same length outside of the stone. Separate the base wires in 2 groups, bending them outwards.

TUTORIALS

22. Separate the woven base wires from the stone. Hold the stone tight between the wire structure and your fingers, then bend each prong to the front, bending them close to the stone.

23. With the help of the chain nose pliers we must push the prongs tightly over the surface of the stone, as shown here and in the next picture.

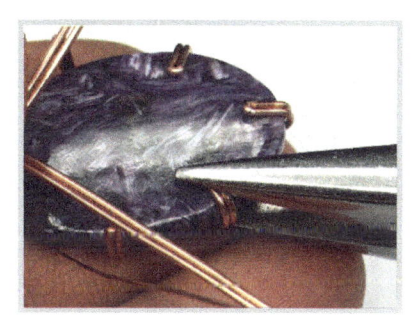

24. Press each prong with the tip of the chain nose pliers, to make sure that they are bent tightly over the stone.

25. Repeat the same steps until all prongs are bent tightly over the surface of the stone, as shown here.

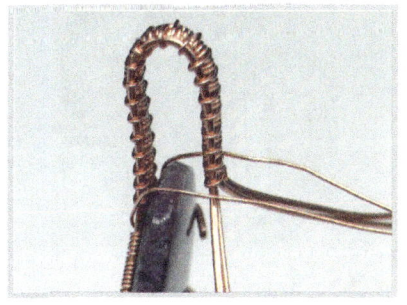

26. Push the woven base wires closer to the top of the stone, then take these 2 weaving wire ends to the front, near the woven base wires.

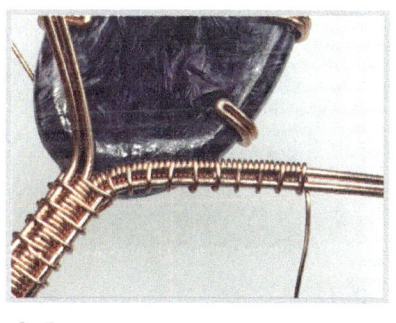

27. Turn the wire structure upside down, then with the weaving wire end on this side make 10 rotations of the 3-1 weave around these 2 base wires.

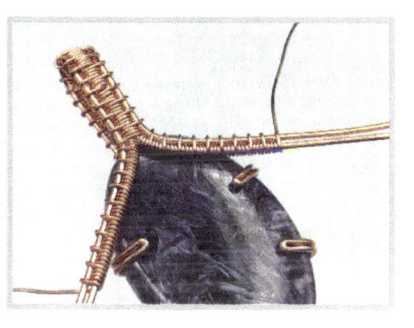

28. Now turn the wire structure back to its original place and repeat the same weaving steps on the other side as well (10 rotations of the 3-1 weave)., as shown here.

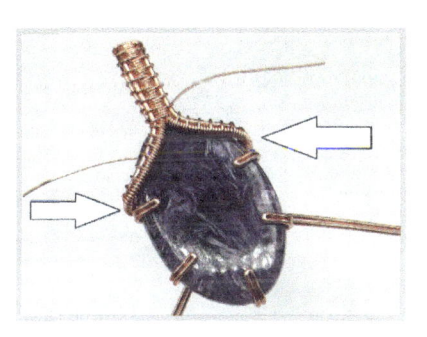

29. On both sides, bend the base wire ends completely behind the stone, as shown here and in the next picture.

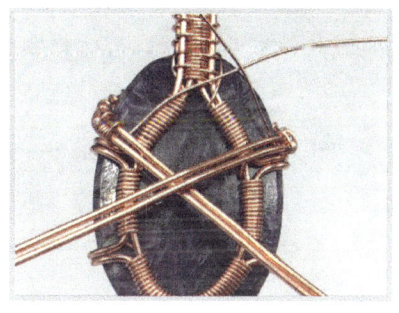

30. Switch to the back view. This is the result we must get. The base wire ends must stay close to the upper prong on each side.

73

TUTORIALS

31. On the right side, take the weaving wire end to the left side under the woven base wires of the prong setting.

32. Pull the weaving wire to the left side direction until it is wrapped tightly under the woven base wires.

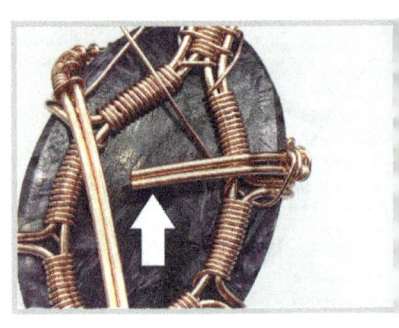

33. Leave a 0.8 cm long end on these 2 base wires on the right side, cut off the extra wire ends.

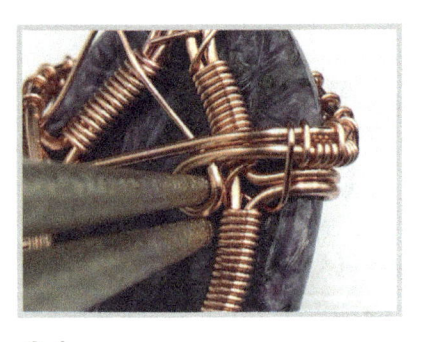

34. Hold the lower wire end tight within the tip of the round nose pliers, then bend it outwards, making a small, closed loop with it, as shown.

35. Wrap the weaving wire 3 times around the upper base wire and the loop, then cut off the extra weaving wire end. Press it with the chain nose pliers to close it.

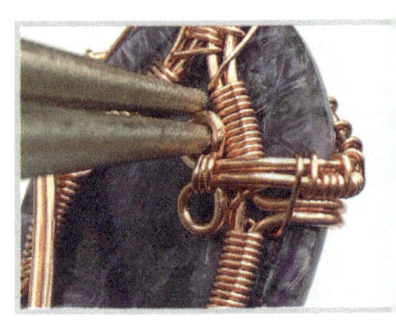

36. Hold the upper wire end tight within the tip of the round nose pliers, then bend it outwards, making a small, closed loop with it, as shown.

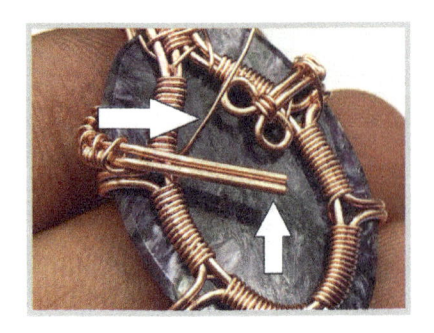

37. Repeat the same steps on the left side. Take the weaving wire to the right side under the woven base wires. Leave a 0.8 cm long end on these 2 base wires, cut off the extra wire ends.

38. Make 2 closed loops with these 2 base wire ends and wrap the weaving wire 3 times around the loops, then cut off the extra wire end.

Switch to the front view.
Your beautiful pendant is ready.

74

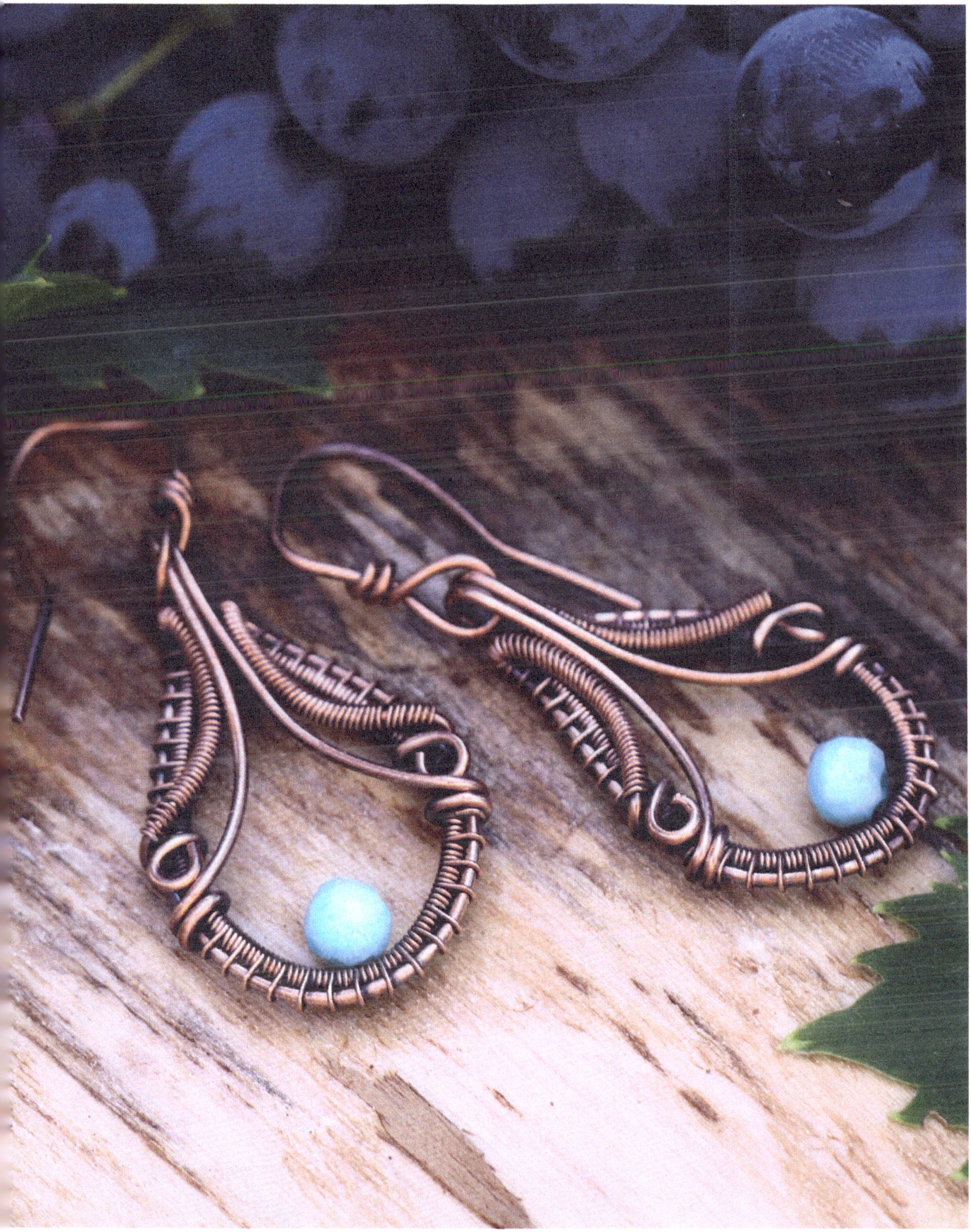

TUTORIALS

Elegance Earrings

These wire wrapped earrings are a very versatile design as you can make them with almost any bead sizes and shapes. The beads I will use are 4 mm big.
Tools needed: chain (or flat) nose pliers, round nose pliers, wire flush cutter
Wires: -20ga (0.8 mm) wire: 4x 8 inches (20 cm), 2x 3 inches (7.5 cm)
         -28ga (0.3 mm) wire: 2x 40 inches (100 cm)

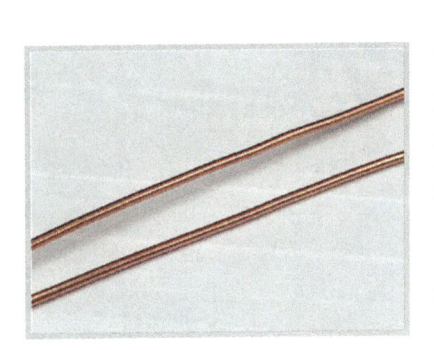

1. First we will make 1 earring. Cut 2 wires of the 20ga (0.8 mm) wire, with the length of 8 inches (20 cm), each. Hold them together with the ends of them aligned.

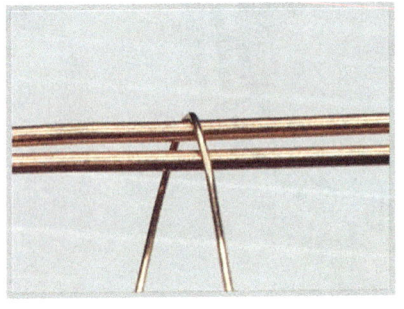

2. Cut a 40 inches (100 cm) long weaving wire. Bend it in half and position the bent center of it around the center of the base wires.

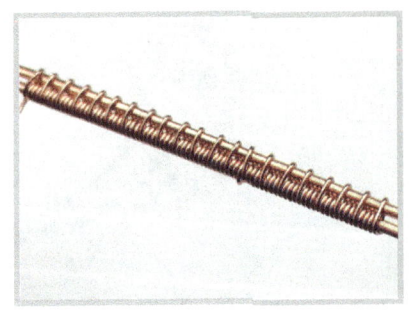

3. Take the right end of the weaving wire, make 20 rotations of the 3-1 weave, as tight as you can. (3 wraps around the lower base wire, 1 wrap around both base wires).

76

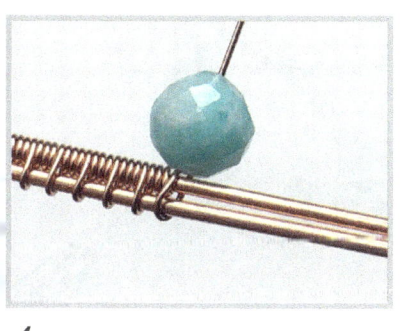

TUTORIALS

4. Turn the wires from the right side to the left side so the woven part is on the left. Add a bead to this other weaving wire end on the center of the wires.

5. Hold the bead on the top, then bend the weaving wire downwards behind it, taking it to the front between the 2 base wires, as shown.

6. With this other weaving wire end, we must make another 20 rotations of the 3-1 weave, this time wrapping it 3 times around the upper base wire and once around both base wires.

7. Bend both sides of the woven base wires upwards, exactly in the same way as shown, until the ends of the woven parts meet at the top.

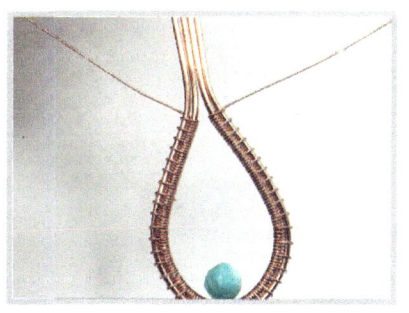

8. Close to the ends of the woven parts, bend all the base wires upwards, making them vertical and parallel, as shown.

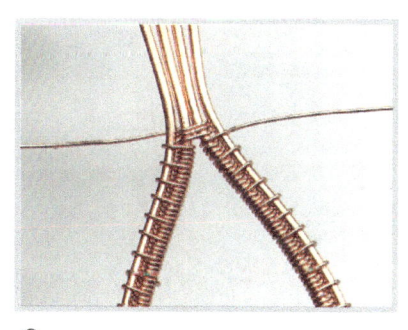

9. Wrap the left weaving wire 3 times around the 2 inner base wires of the 4 wires, to connect the 2 sides of the wire structure.

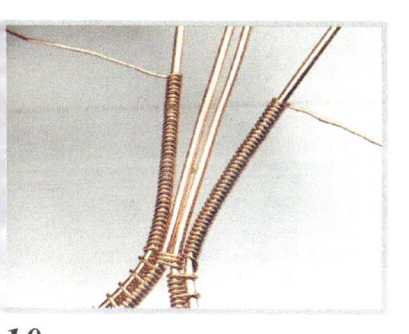

10. On both sides, wrap the weaving wires 40 times around the outer base wires, as tight as you can. We call this process coiling the weaving wire around the base wire.

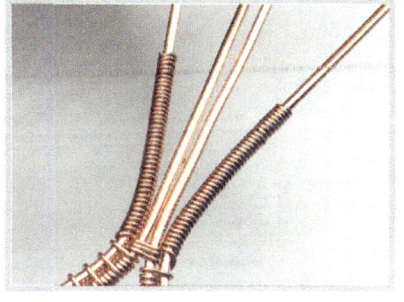

11. Now cut off the weaving wire ends on both sides, then press the ends of them with the chain nose pliers until they are completely closed.

12. Bend these coiled base wires completely downwards, exactly in the same way as shown here.

77

TUTORIALS

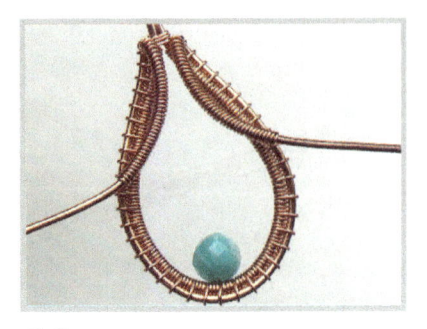

13. Bend these coiled base wires to the sides, making a little curved part with them and positioning the ends of the coiled part over the woven base wires.

14. On the right side, hold the coiled base wire tight between your fingers, then bend the base wire end in a way to take it to the front through the center of the wire structure.

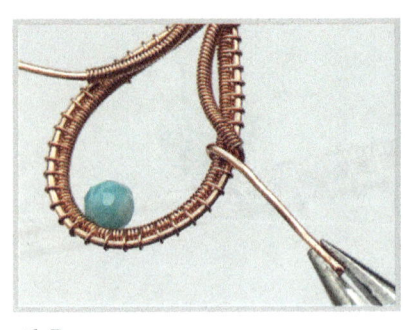

15. With the help of the chain nose pliers, pull the wire end to the right-side direction, making a tight wrap with this base wire around the woven wires.

16. Leave a 1 cm long end on this base wire, cut off the extra end of it.

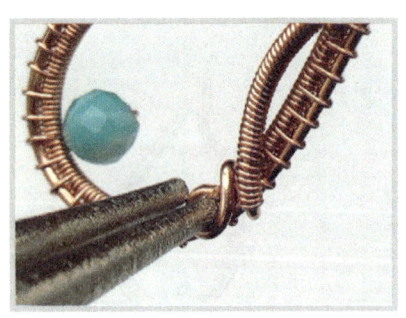

17. Hold the wire end within the tip of the round nose pliers, then bend it inwards, making a small, closed loop with it.

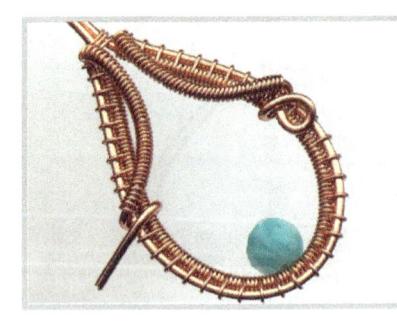

18. We must repeat the same bending steps on the left side as well. Leave a 1 cm long base wire end, cut off the extra end of it.

19. Now bend the wire end inwards with the tip of the round nose pliers, to make a small, closed loop with it.

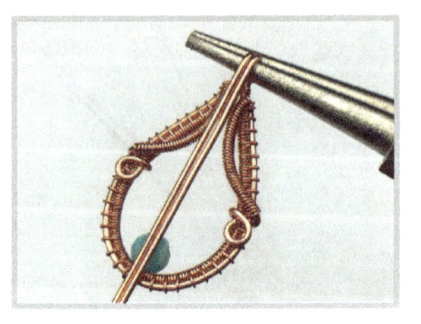

20. At the top of the wire structure, hold both inner base wires tight within the round nose pliers. Bend the wires completely downwards.

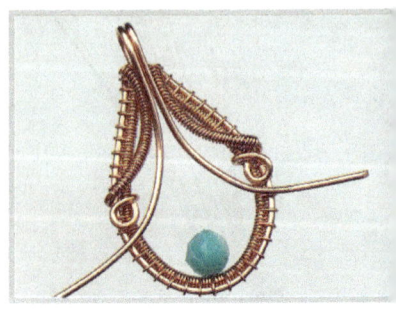

21. Now bend these wires to the sides, making a small curve with them, and positioning them below the loops we recently made.

78

TUTORIALS

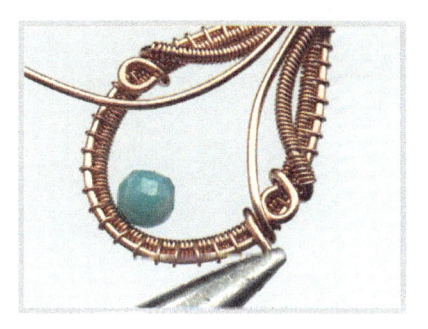

22. Repeat the same bending steps as we did with the previous wire on this side, making a tight wrap with it around the woven wires.

23. Leave a 0.4 cm long end on this wire. Cut off the extra wire, then bend the short end of it completely backwards. Press it with the chain nose pliers, until it is completely closed.

24. Repeat the same steps on the left side as well, wrapping the wire around the woven base wires. Leave a 0.4 cm long end on it, cut off the extra wire end.

25. Bend the short wire end completely backwards, then press it to close it. Switch to the back view and double check if both wire ends are closed.

26. For the ear wire cut a 3 inches (7.5 cm) long base wire of the 20ga (0.8 mm) wire. Repeat the steps learned previously, to bend the wire until shown on this picture.

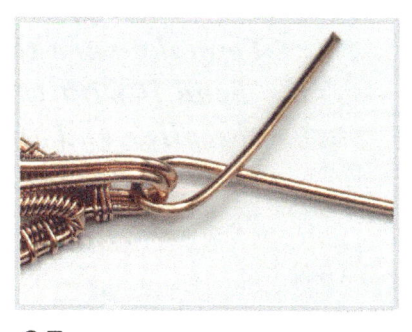

27. Insert the bent ear wire into the space at the top of the earring, then continue to bend the wire ends as learned previously.

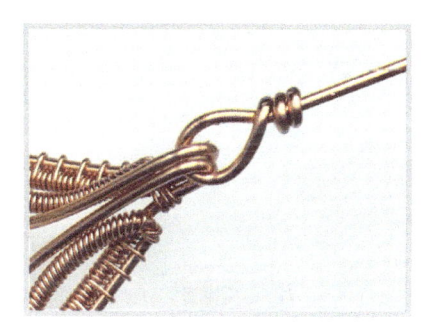

28. Continue with the previously learned steps, to wrap the shorter wire end around the longer one.

29. Continue to bend the longer wire end to finish the ear wire, as we learned. Use a nail file to make the end of the ear wire smooth.

30. Repeat all the steps one more time, to create a second earring.

Your earrings are ready.

79

Tip:

To make sure that we do not damage the base wire while we bend it with the tip of the chain nose pliers, we can cover the plier ends with soft tape, so we can keep our wires safe from any mark while we practice how to bend them to their correct shape.

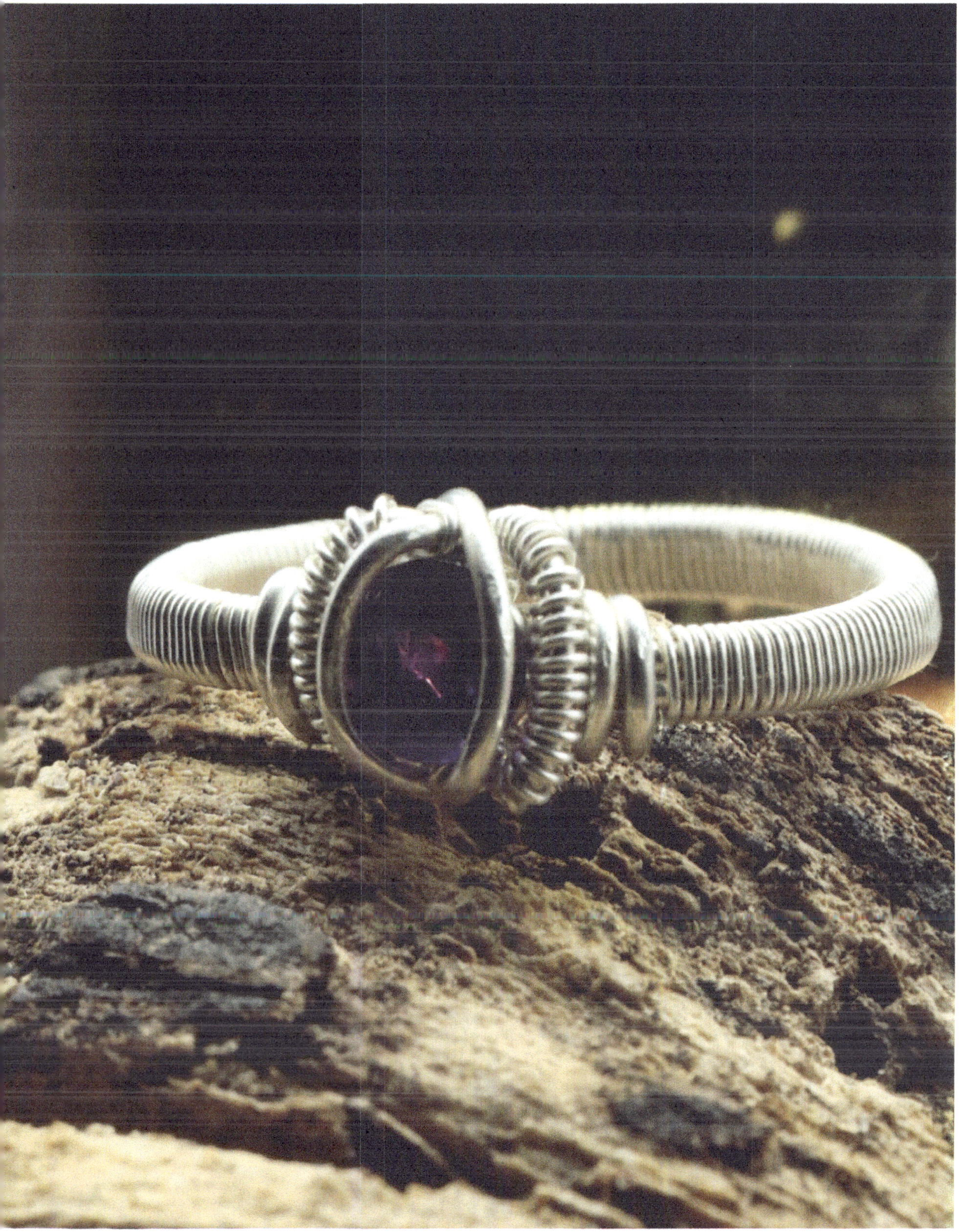

TUTORIALS

Simple Crystal Ring

The first jewelry has been made from found objects, such as shells, bones, wood, and carved stones. Many of th
antient jewelry pieces were decorated with gemstones, like emerald and topaz. In the 1800's people started t
create crystals, which were affordable alternatives to diamonds, and everyone could afford to wear a crysta
jewelry. Crystals are a very elegant addition to any jewelry, and they can be used for wedding jewelry too. Toda
we have endless options to add gemstones and crystals to our handmade jewelry.
In this tutorial we will learn how to set a small, faceted gemstone tightly into an elegant and delicate ring.
Tools needed: chain (or flat) nose pliers, wire flush cutter, ring mandrel (or wooden dowel)
Wires: -20ga (0.8 mm): 2x max. 6 inches (15 cm)
  -26ga (0.4 mm) wire: 1x max. 50 inches (125 cm), 1x 10 inches (25 cm)
  -round shaped faceted, pointed back crystal between 5-6 mm big

TUTORIALS

1. Take any wire, wrap it once around the ring mandrel, over the ring size you wish to make. Cut off the extra wire end. This wire measures the length of the ring circumference.

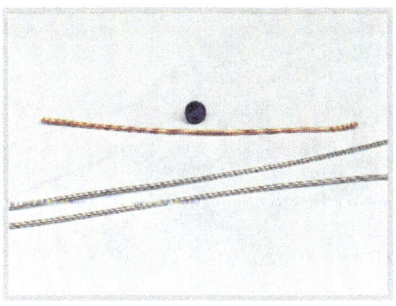

2. Straighten the ring circumference wire, then cut 2 base wires with the length of 2x times the ring circumference wire. In my case I take 2 base wires of 5 inches (12.5 cm) long.

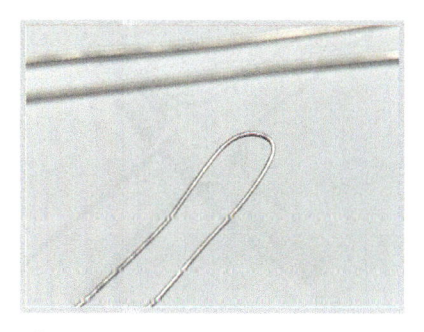

3. Cut a 40 inches (100 cm) long weaving wire of the 26ga (0.4 mm) wire. Bend it in half, as shown here.

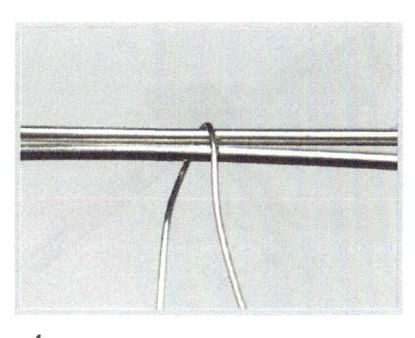

4. Hold the base wires together. Make sure the ends of them are aligned. Position the bent center of the weaving wire around the center of the base wires.

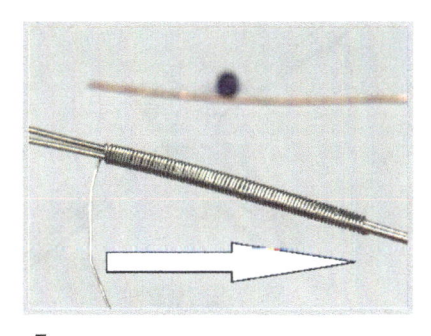

5. Coil the right end of the weaving wire around both base wires, until the coiled part has the length of a half ring circumference. Cut off the extra weaving wire.

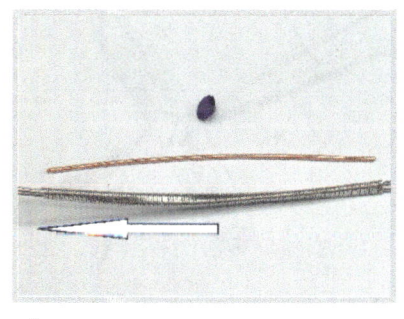

6. Repeat the same steps on the left side as well, so the coiled part has the same length as the ring circumference measuring wire, as shown here.

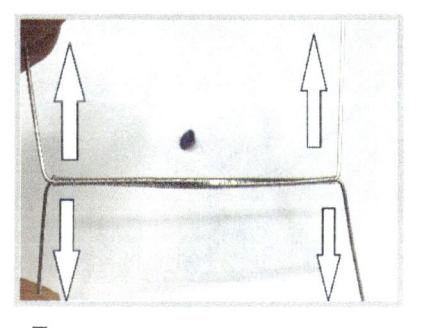

7. On both sides, where the coiled part ends, bend the upper wire completely upwards and the lower wire completely downwards, as shown with the arrows.

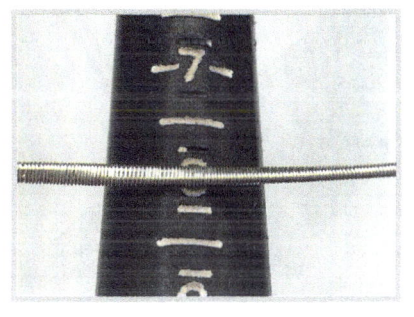

8. Position the center of the coiled part over the ring mandrel (or wooden dowel).

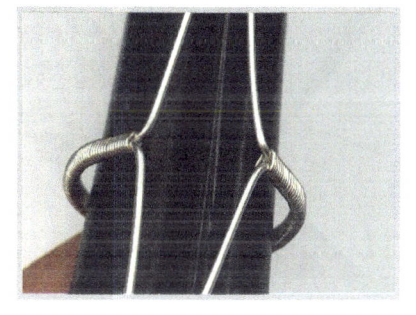

9. Bend both sides of the ring all around the mandrel, until the wire ends meet on the other side of it, as shown.

83

TUTORIALS

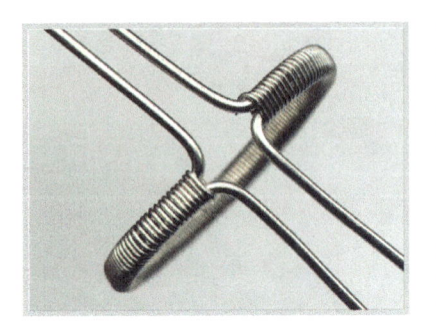

10. Separate the ring from the mandrel. If necessary, straighten the wire ends and position the 2 sides of the ring closer.

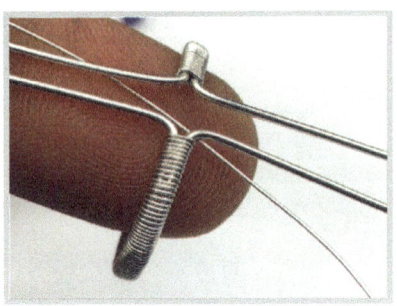

11. Cut a 10 inches (25 cm) long weaving wire of the 26ga (0.4 mm) wire. Position the center of this weaving wire behind the center of the ring on this side.

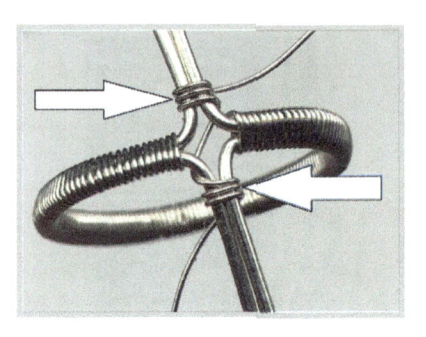

12. Wrap both ends of this weaving wire 3 times around the upper and the lower base wires, to connect them.

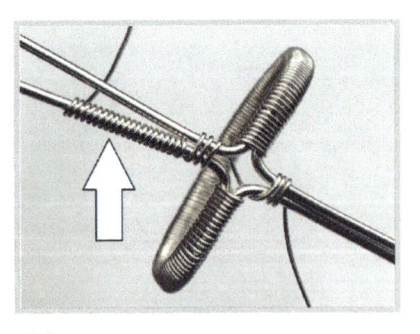

13. On the upper side, coil the weaving wire 20 times around the left base wire, as tight as possible.

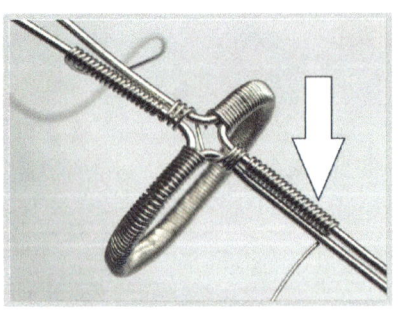

14. On the lower side, coil the weaving wire 20 times around the right base wire, as tight as you can.

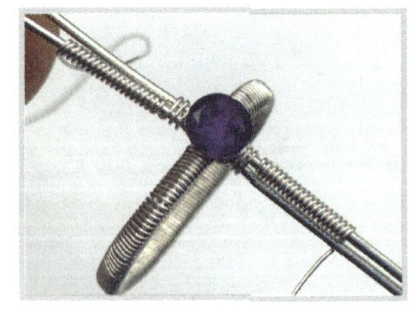

15. Position your small stone over the center of the ring, making sure that the pointed back of the stone sits well in between the base wires.

16. Position the ring mandrel inside the ring, then hold the stone tightly and bend all the base wires completely to the front.

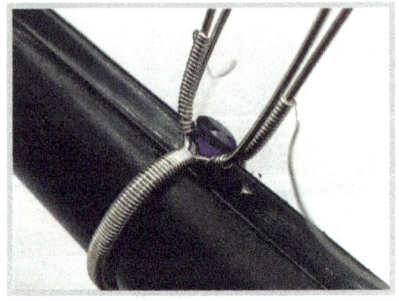

17. This is the same step from the other side. Make sure that the wires are bent tightly, and they are positioned close to the upper and the lower side of the stone.

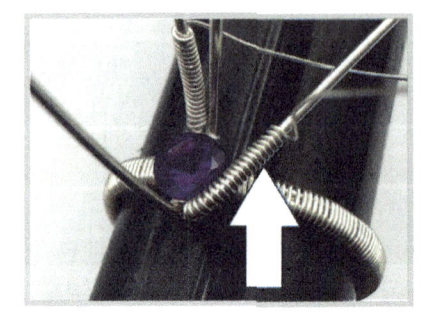

18. Take the coiled base wire from the lower side, bend it upwards, bending it tightly over the right lower side of the stone.

TUTORIALS

19. Take the coiled base wire from the upper side, bend it downwards, bending it tightly over the left upper side of the stone.

20. Now we must repeat the same bending steps with the other upper and lower base wire as well, bending them to the opposite directions over the stone.

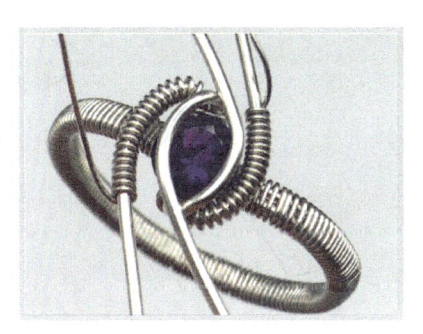

21. Separate the ring from the mandrel and if necessary, adjust the position of the wires until they hold the stone tightly.

22. Hold the stone tightly, then take the right lower base wire to the front on the right side of the stone, behind the ring. Bend it tightly downwards.

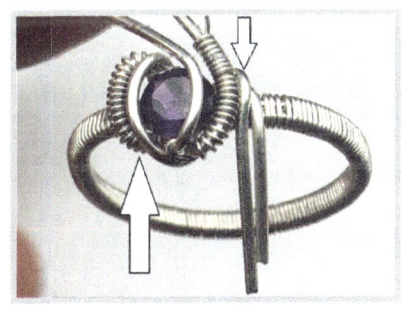

23. Cut off the extra weaving wire end on this side. Repeat the same bending steps with the coiled base wire too. Make sure that these 2 wires hold the left side of the stone tightly.

24. Turn the ring upside down and repeat the same bending steps with the other 2 base wires as well. The stone must stay very tight inside the setting.

25. Leave a 0.3 cm long end on the base wires, on both sides. Cut off the extra wire ends.

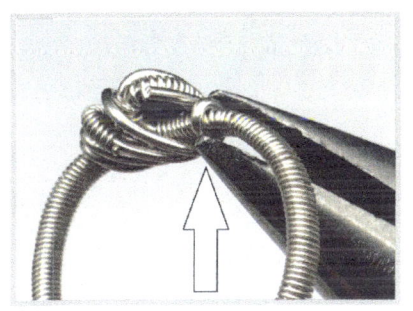

26. One by one, bend the short wire end backwards, with the help of the chain nose pliers, then press them until they are completely closed behind the ring band.

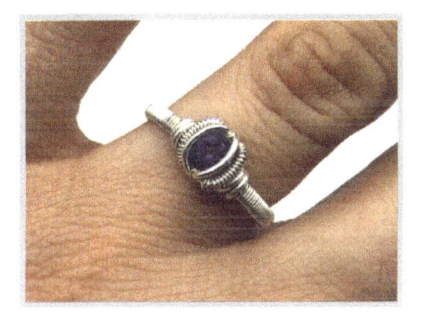

Once each wire end has been bent tightly backwards, make sure that they are completely closed.
Your beautiful crystal ring is ready.

85

Tip:

To give an antiqued color to our finished jewelry, we can use Liver of Sulphur gel. This patina is used once the jewelry is finished. Mix 1-2 drops of this gel with warm water, then keep your jewelry in this mix until it gets dark (almost black). Remove it from the mix, rinse it with clean water, then rub it with steel wool, to remove all the dark patina, until your jewelry gets a light brownish color.

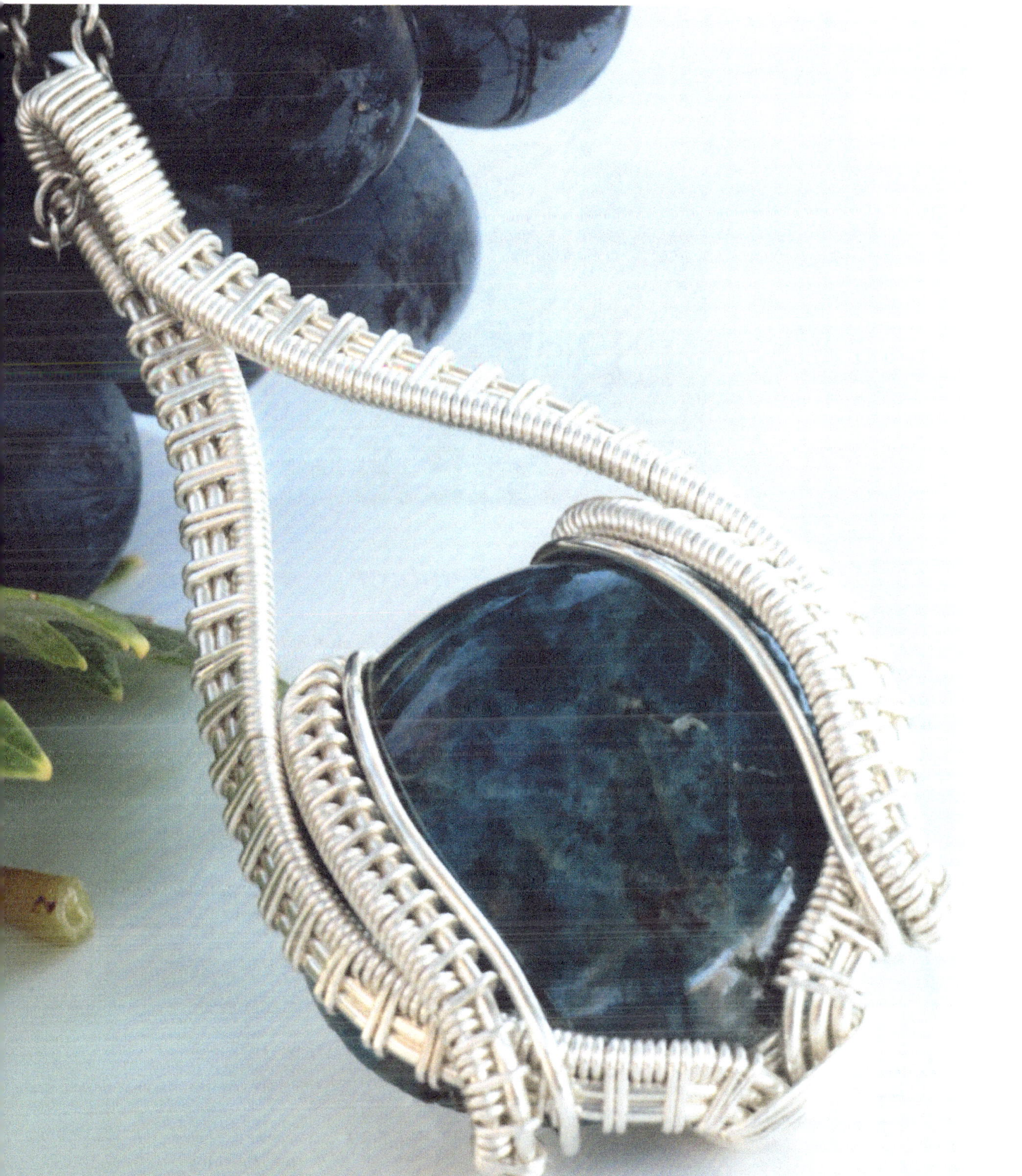

TUTORIALS

Grace Pendant

This tutorial will teach you how to wrap round, flat back cabochon, decorating it with 2 weaving techniques we learned previously. We will need a round cabochon between 20-25 mm big.
Tools needed: chain (or flat) nose pliers, round nose plier, wire flush cutter
Wires: -20ga (0.8 mm) wire: 3x 12 inches (30 cm)
       -26ga (0.4 mm) wire: 2x 60 inches (150 cm)

1. Materials and tools for this project are shown on this picture. The stone I chose to use for this pendant is 22 mm big.

2. Cut 3 base wires of the 20ga (0.8 mm) wire, with the length of 12 inches (30 cm), each. Cut a 60 inches (150 cm) long 26ga (0.4 mm) weaving wire. Bend it in half, as shown.

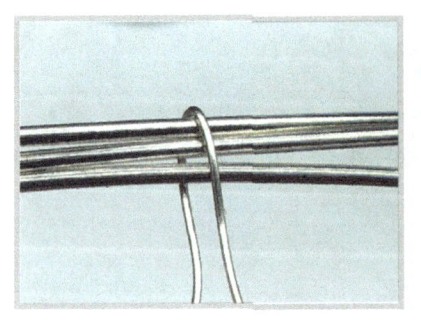

3. Hold the 3 base wires together, making sure that the ends of them are aligned. Position the bent center of the weaving wire around the center of the lower base wire.

88

TUTORIALS

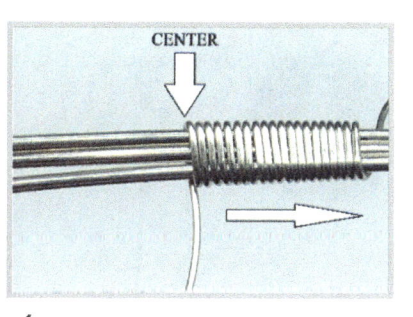

4. Take the front end of the weaving wire, wrap it 20 times around all 3 base wires, as tight as you can. I flattened the wrapped part with the chain nose pliers, to make it firm.

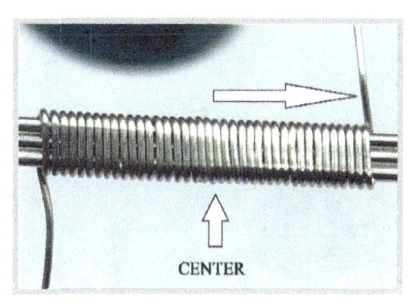

5. Turn the wire structure from the right side to the left side, clockwise. Take the other weaving wire end and make 20 wraps with this one too.

6. With the right end of the weaving wire make 23 rotations of the 3-2 weave, as tight as possible.

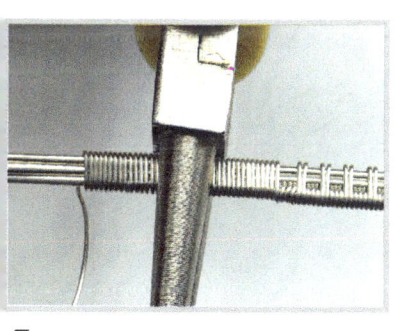

7. Hold the center of the first woven part you made around all 3 base wires, tight within the bottom of the round nose pliers.

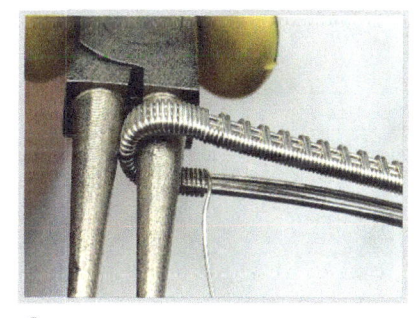

8. With the help of the pliers, bend the left half of the base wires to the right-side direction, exactly in the same way as shown.

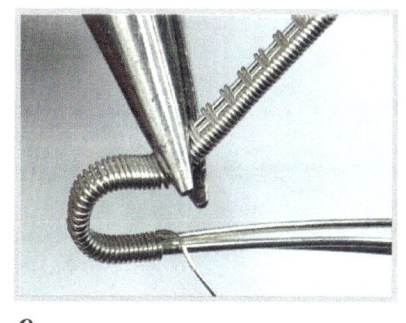

9. On the upper side, hold the initial part of the 3-2 weave tight within the tip of the chain nose pliers, bend the woven base wires slightly upwards.

10. Make 23 rotations of the 3-2 weave with the other weaving wire end, weaving upside down (3 wraps around the upper base wire, 2 wraps around all 3 base wires).

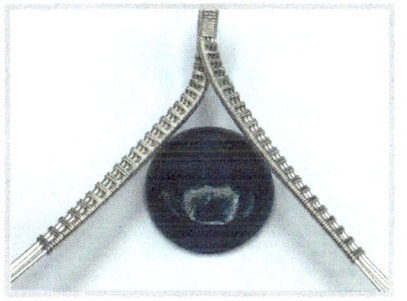

11. Position the wires in vertical as shown. On the top, push the bent part of the 3-2 weave over the other side of the base wires, to close the bail. Separate the 2 sides of the woven base wires, as shown here.

12. Cut off both weaving wire ends. Bend the base wires all around the stone circumference. The base wires must cross over each other at the bottom center of the stone, where the woven parts end.

89

TUTORIALS

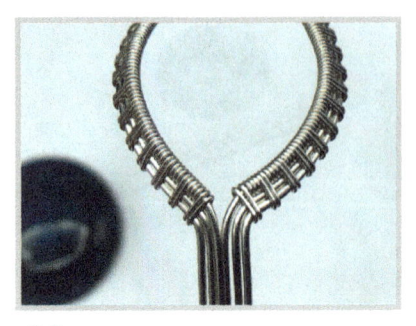

13. *At this point, bend all the 6 base wire ends completely downwards, then push them slightly backwards, as shown here and on the next picture.*

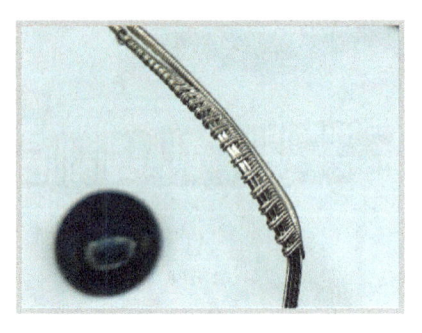

14. *This is the result we must get from the left side view of the wire structure.*

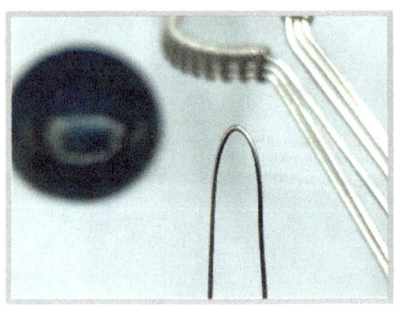

15. *Cut another weaving wire of the 26ga (0.6 mm) wire, with the length of 60 inches (150 cm). Bend it in half.*

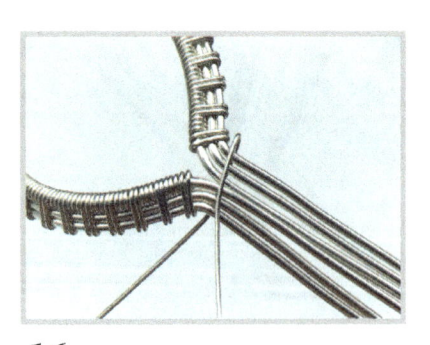

16. *Position the bent center of this weaving wire around the 6 base wires, close to the bent part of them.*

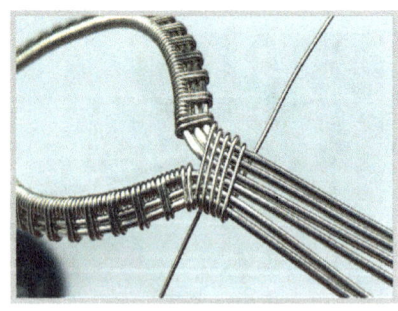

17. *Wrap the front weaving wire end 5 times around all 6 base wires.*

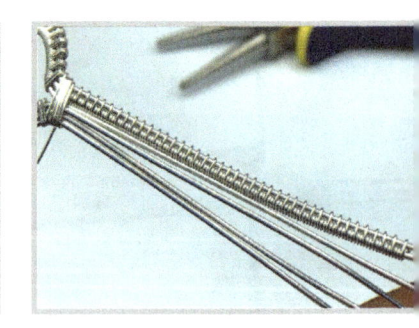

18. *With the same weaving wire end make 40 rotations of the 2-1 weave around the 2 upper base wires (from this point of view).*

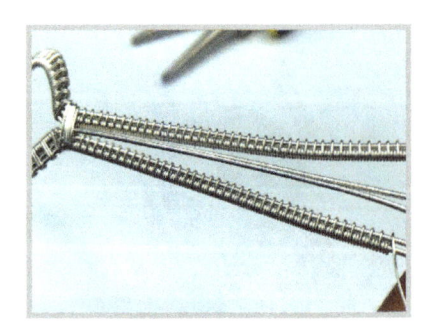

19. *With the other weaving wire end make 40 rotations of the 2-1 weave around the 2 lower base wires. You can make this weave in the opposite way or as it is on the upper side.*

20. *Switch to the back view of the wire structure. Position the stone inside the wires, then bend all the 6 base wires toward yourself.*

21. *Hold the stone tight between your fingers and the wires. Take the woven base wires from the right side, bend them in a way to take them to the front through the wire structure.*

90

TUTORIALS

22. Pull the wire ends completely upwards until they are positioned tightly over the back of the stone, as shown. Straighten the woven wires as much as possible.

23. Take the next base wire from the right side, repeat the same steps to take it to the front.

24. Now repeat the same steps with the other wires as well, as shown. All 6 wires must be positioned tightly over the back of the stone.

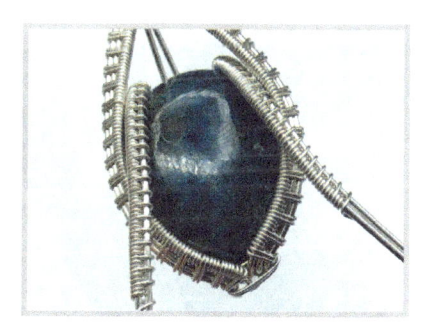

25. On the front, bend the woven base wires downwards, bending them tightly over the stone, then move them slightly to the sides.

26. On the right side, bend the end of the woven part outwards, making a little curve with it, as shown.

27. Repeat the same step on the left side as well, then bend the ends of these woven base wires backwards, over the back of the stone.

28. Take the next base wire from the right side, bend it downwards then backwards exactly in the same way as the woven base wires are bent, positioning it close to these woven wires.

29. With the other base wire we must repeat the same steps on the left side as well, as shown here.

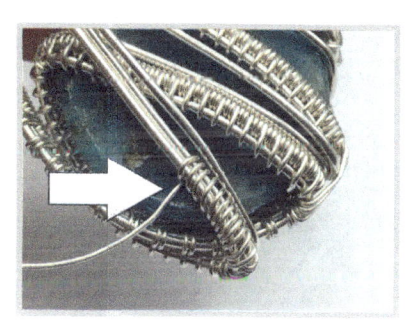

30. Switch to the back view. On the left side, wrap the weaving wire 12 times around the ends of the woven base wires.

TUTORIALS

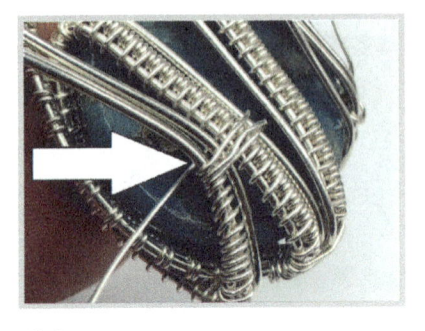

31. Bend all 3 wires slightly to position them close to the woven base wires over the back of the stone. Wrap the weaving wire 3 times around all these wires shown with the arrow, to connect them.

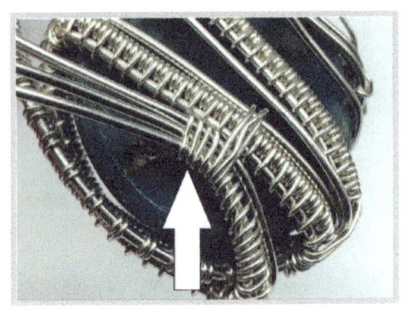

32. Wrap the weaving wire 3 times around the 3 base wire ends, then cut off the extra weaving wire end. Press the end of it with the tip of the chain nose pliers until it is completely closed.

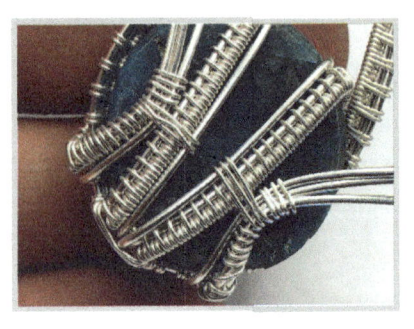

33. Repeat the same weaving steps on the right side as well then cut off the extra weaving wire end here too.

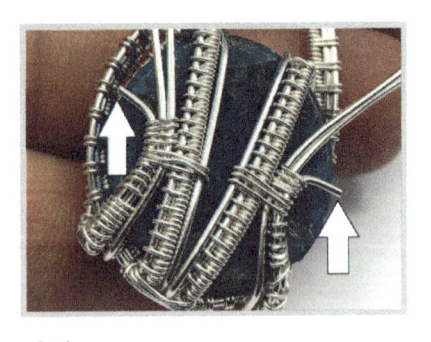

34. On both sides bend the lower base wire end to the side. Leave a 0.4 cm long end on them, cut off the extra wire ends.

35. On the right side, with the tip of the chain nose pliers, bend the short wire end completely downwards, then press it until it is closed.

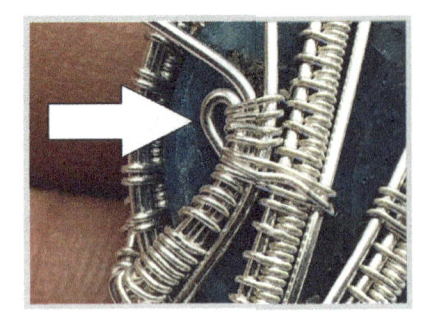

36. Repeat the same step on the left side as well, to close the short wire end, as shown.

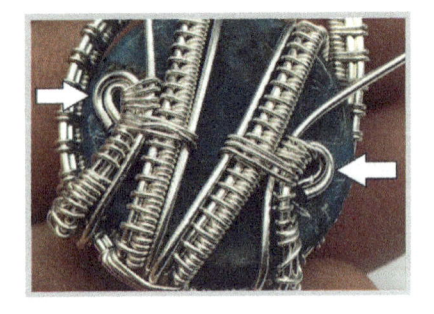

37. Leave a 0.5 cm long end on the next base wire on both sides, then repeat the same steps as we did with the lower base wire ends, to close them.

38. Leave a 0.8 cm long end on the upper base wire on both sides, then repeat the same steps as we did with the other base wire ends, to close them completely, as shown with the arrows.

Switch to the front view. Your beautiful pendant is ready.

TIP: Try this design using an oval shaped cabochon in horizontal position.

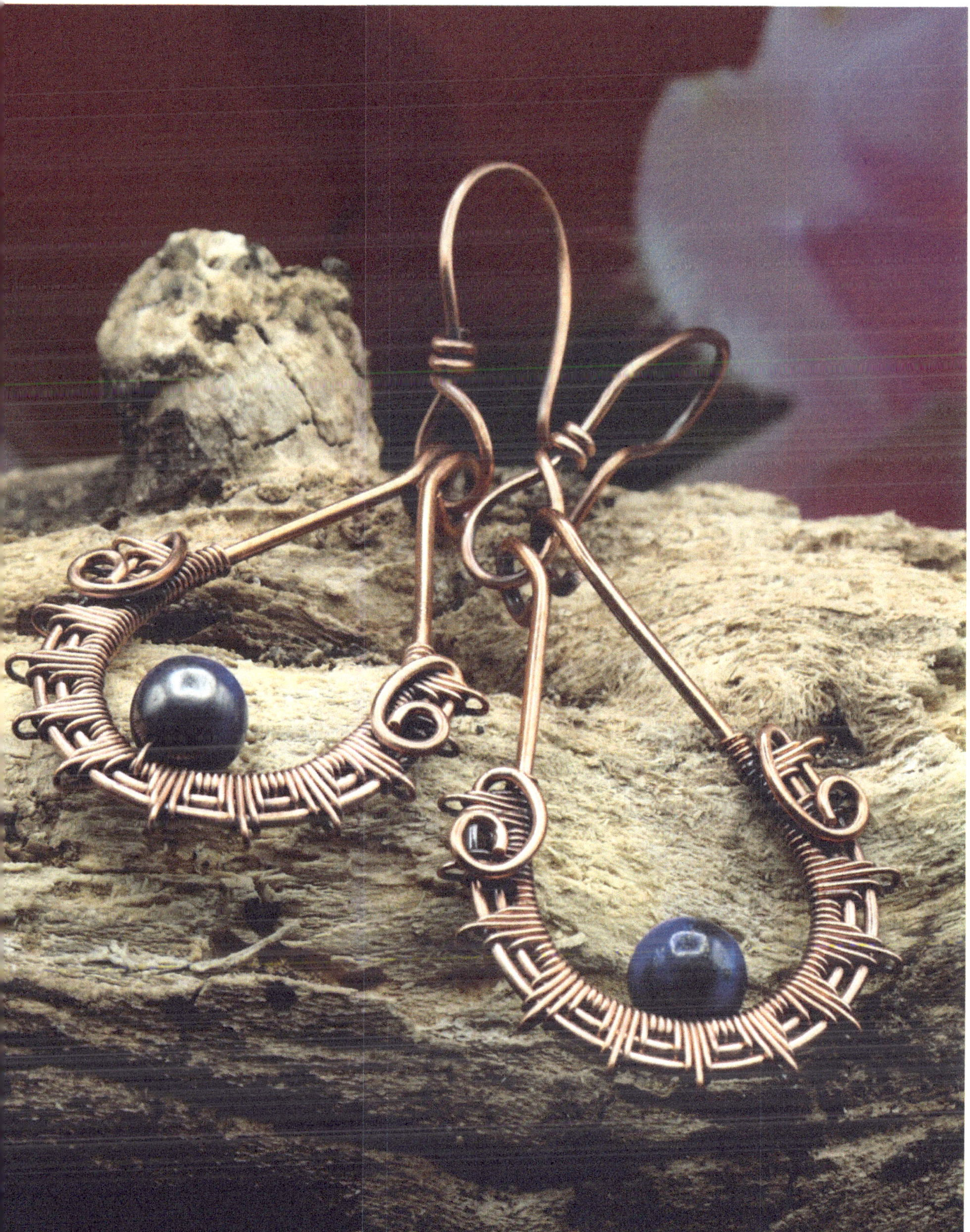

TUTORIALS

Sun Weave Earrings

This tutorial will teach you how to give an extra touch to this sun weave, with the addition of a simple step. For these earrings we can use 2 beads between 4-8 mm big, each.
Tools needed: chain (or flat) nose pliers, round nose plier, wire flush cutter
Wires: -18ga (1 mm) wire: 2x 6 inches (15 cm)   -20ga (0.8 mm) wire: 6x 4 inches (10 cm)
       -26ga (0.4 mm) wire: 2x 32 inches (80 cm)

1. Materials and tools for this project are shown on this picture. For these earrings I will use two 6 mm beads.

2. First we will make the ear wires as we learned in the techniques section.

3. For 1 earring cut 6 inches (15 cm) long 18ga (1 mm) wire and 3 pieces of 4 inches (10 cm) long 20ga (0.8 mm) wire. Position the 18ga (1 mm) wire below the other wires, with the center of them aligned.

TUTORIALS

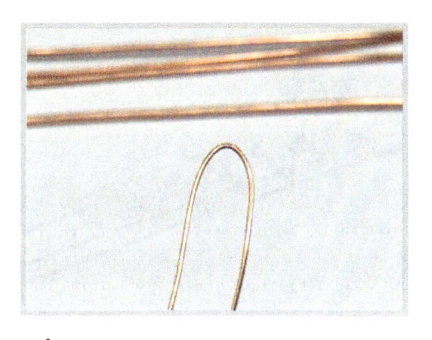

4. Cut a 32 inches (80 cm) long weaving wire of the 26ga (0.4 mm) wire. Bend it in half, as shown here.

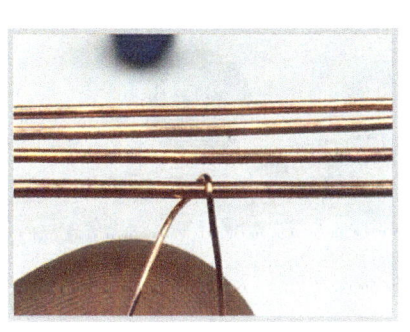

5. Make sure that the center of the 4 base wires is aligned, then position the bent center of the weaving wire around the center of the lower, 18ga (1 mm) base wire.

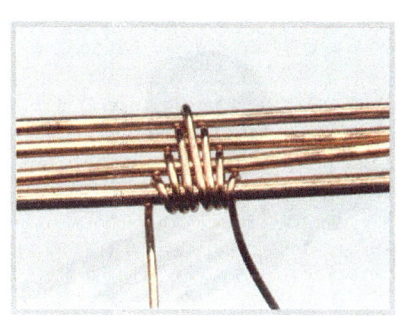

6. With the front end of the weaving wire, make 1 rotation of the sun weave, as shown here.

7. With the help of the chain nose pliers, compress the woven part, pushing it slowly to the left side direction.

8. Now flatten the woven part, pressuring it with the chain nose pliers, as shown here. We will repeat these steps after every single rotation.

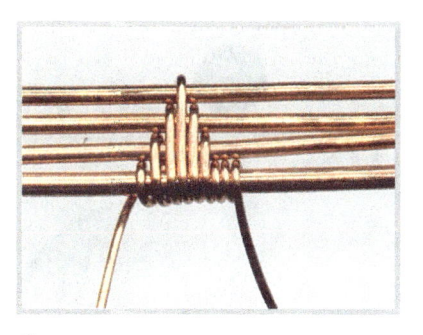

9. Now wrap the weaving wire 3 times around the lower base wire, as tight as possible.

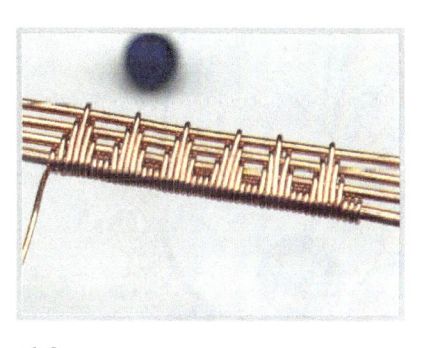

10. Make another 5 rotations of the sun weave. Cut off the extra weaving wire end on this side. Press the short weaving wire end with the tip of the chain nose pliers, until it is completely closed.

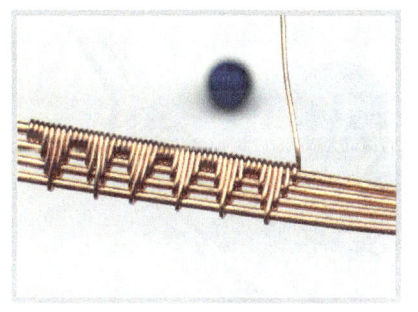

11. Turn the wire structure from the right side to the left side, clockwise, so the recently made woven part is on the left side from the center of the base wires.

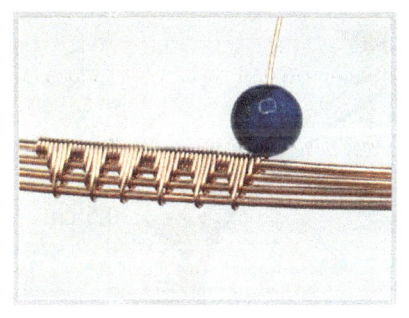

12. Add your bead to the other weaving wire end on the top, positioning the bead close to the base wires.

95

TUTORIALS

13. At the top of the base wire, hold the bead tight between your fingers, then bend the weaving wire end downwards behind the bead, and take it to the front below the upper base wire.

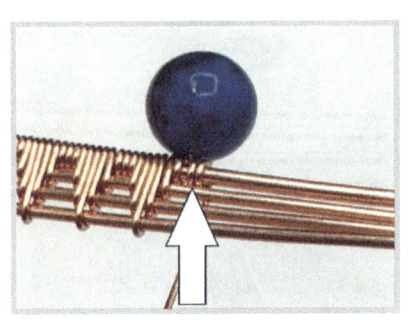

14. Now wrap it 2 times around the upper base wire, as tight as you can, so the bead remains firm on the top.

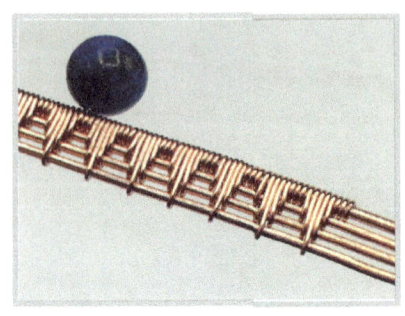

15. With this other weaving wire end we must make another 6 rotations of the sun weave, weaving upside down as tight as possible. Then, cut off the extra weaving wire end.

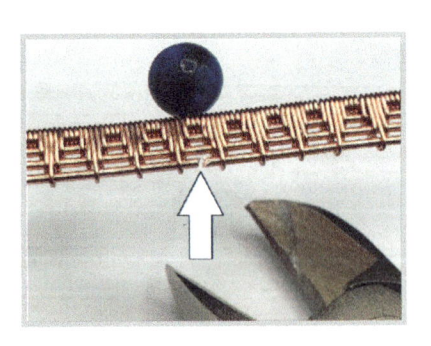

16. Once the woven part is finished, at the center of the wire structure, cut the lower base wire of the sun weave, as shown with the arrow.

17. Very slowly, from the 2 sides, pull out the lower base wire from the weave. This is the result we must get.

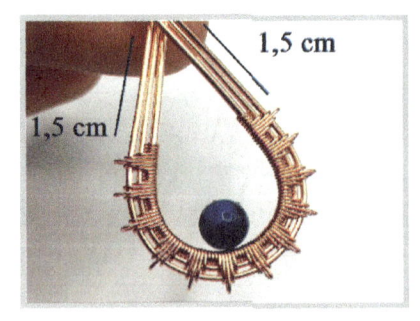

18. Slowly, bend the woven base wires into a teardrop shape, in a way that they cross over each other at a 1.5 cm distance from the end of the woven part.

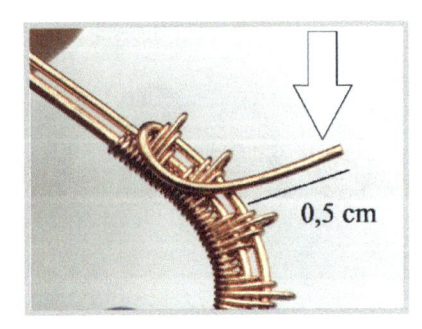

19. On the right side, bend the right base wire downwards then outwards. Leave a 0.5 cm long end on it, cut off the extra wire end.

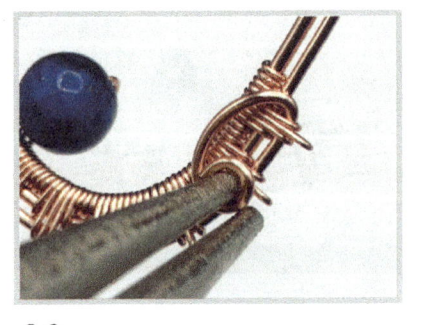

20. Hold the wire end with the tip of the round nose pliers, then bend it inwards, making a small, closed loop with it, positioning this loop over the woven part.

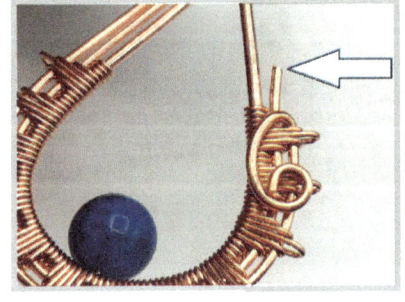

21. Leave a 0.3 cm long end on the next base wire, cut off the extra end of it.

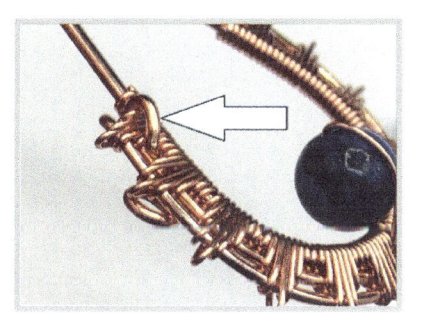

TUTORIALS

22. Switch to the back view. With the tip of the chain nose pliers, bend this short wire end over the woven part then press it until it is completely closed.

23. Let's repeat the same steps on the left side too. Bend the outer base wire downwards, then outwards. Leave a 0.5 cm long end on it, cut off the extra wire end.

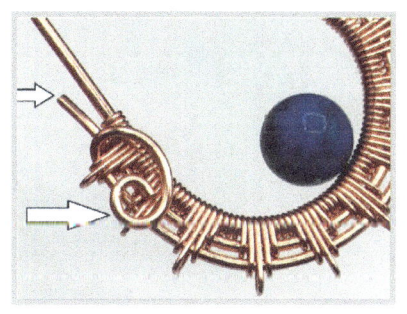

24. Bend the wire end inwards to make a closed loop with it. Leave a 0.3 cm long end on the next base wire, cut off the extra wire end.

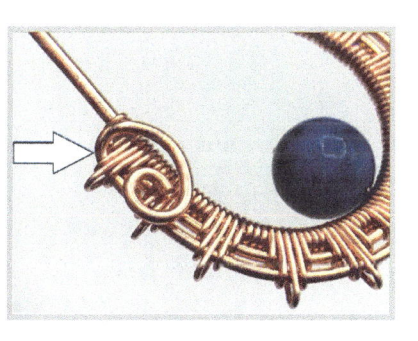

25. Bend the short wire end completely backwards, then press it until it is completely closed on the back.

26. At the top, where the base wire ends cross over each other at a 1,5 cm distance from the end of the woven part, bend them completely upwards.

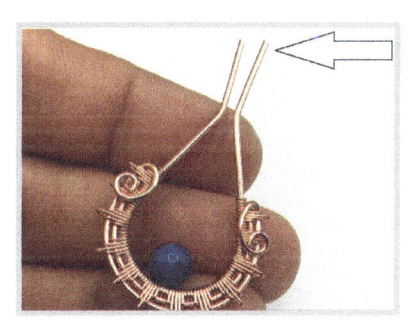

27. Leave a 1 cm long end on both wires, cut off the extra ends of them.

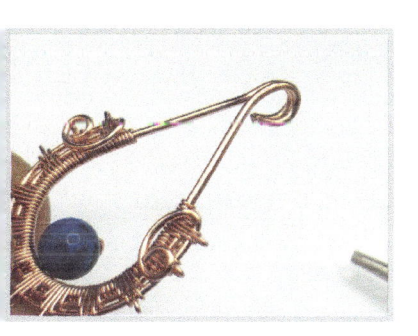

28. Hold the wire ends with the center of the round nose pliers, bend them backwards, making an open loop with these wire ends.

29. Insert these open loops into the loop of the ear wire, then one by one close them with the help of the chain nose pliers, as shown here.

30. Insert these open loops into the loop of the ear wire, then one by one close them with the help of the chain nose pliers, as shown here.

97

Tip:

Jewelry storage:

We can decide to leave our copper jewelry bright, or we can use patina to give an antiqued look. In both cases copper can get slightly darker with the time due to natural oxidation process. To avoid this, we can keep our jewelry in a zip lock bag, which can be completely closed, and the air does not get in. In this way we can keep our jewelry shiny for a longer time.

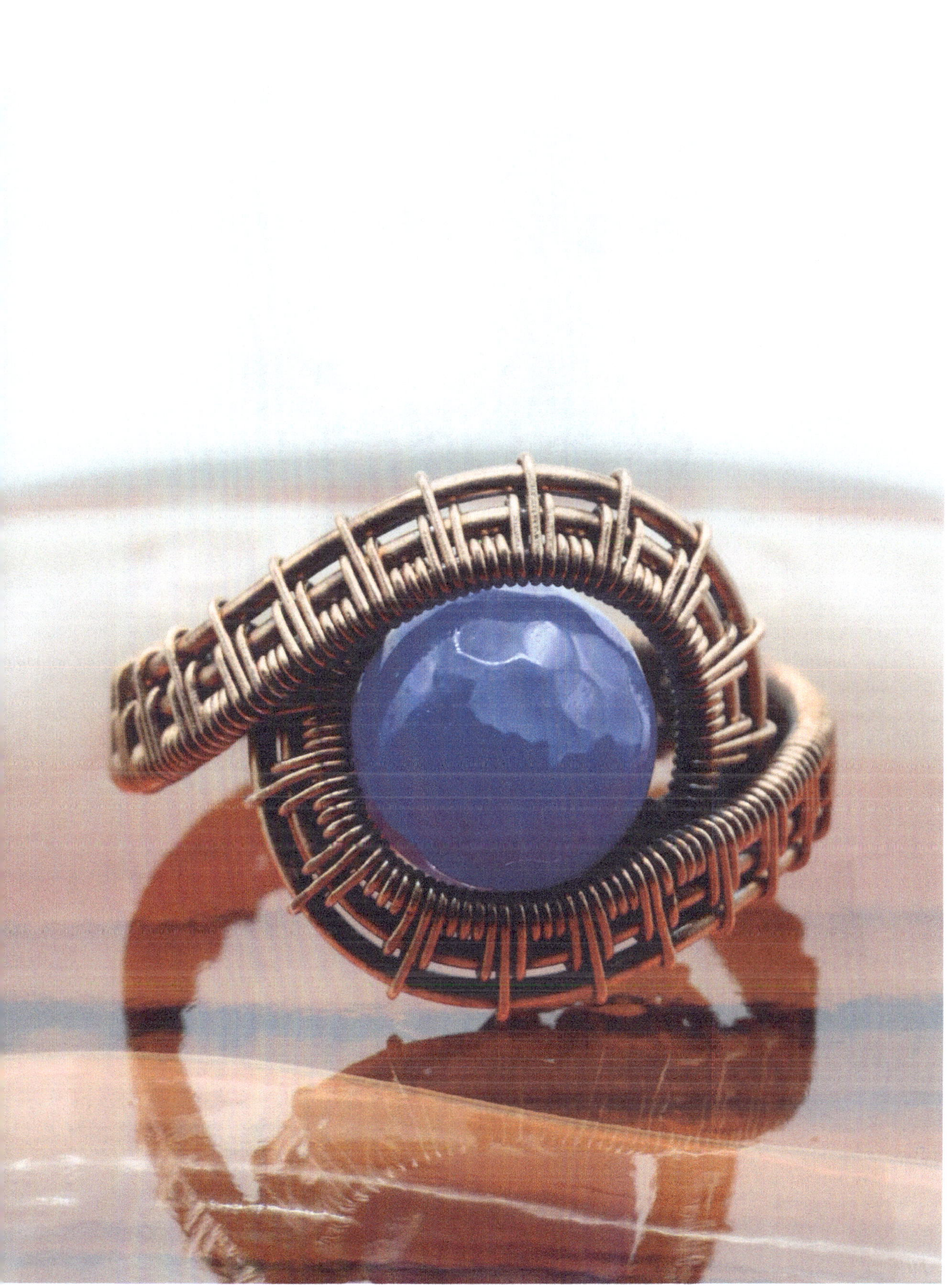

TUTORIALS

Milky Way Ring

Learn how to make a beautiful woven ring with a focal bead, incorporating a previously learned weaving technique. We will need a 10 mm or 8 mm big bead for this tutorial. I will take a 10 mm big bead.
Tools needed: chain (or flat) nose pliers, round nose pliers, wire cutter, ring mandrel (or wooden dowel)
Wires: -18ga (1 mm) OR 20ga (0.8 mm) wire: 3x 8 inches (20 cm)
        -26ga (0.4 mm) wire: 1x 68 inches (170 cm)

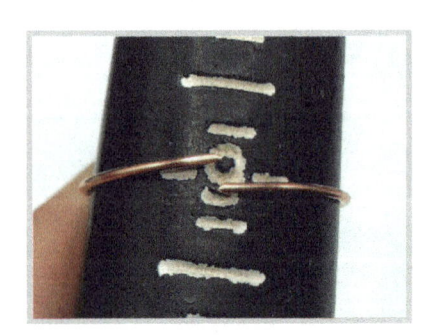

1. Take any wire, wrap it once around the ring mandrel, over the ring size you wish to make. Cut off the extra wire end. This wire measures the length of the ring circumference.

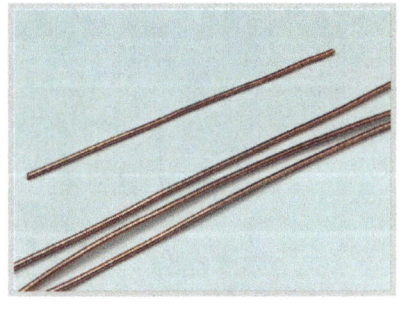

2. Straighten this ring circumference measuring wire, then cut 3 base wires with the length of 8 inches (20 cm), each. I will use 18ga (1 mm) base wire for this ring.

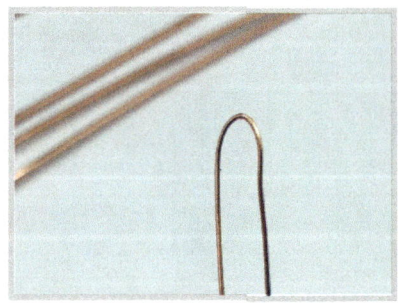

3. Cut a 68 inches (170 cm) long weaving wire of the 26ga (0.4 mm) wire. Bend it in half, as shown here.

100

TUTORIALS

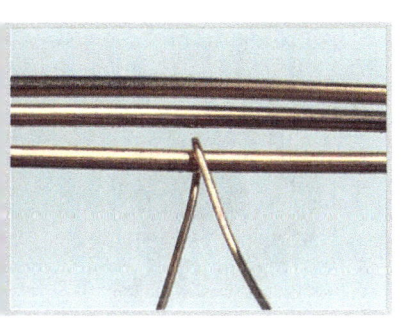

4. Hold all 3 base wires together, making sure that the ends of them are aligned. Position the bent center of the weaving wire around the center of the lower base wire.

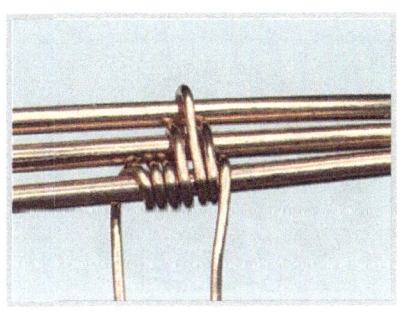

5. Make 1 rotation of the Sun weave, following the previously learned weaving steps, but incorporating only 3 base wires.

6. With the help of the chain nose pliers, compress the woven part as much as possible. In this way the weave will look much better.

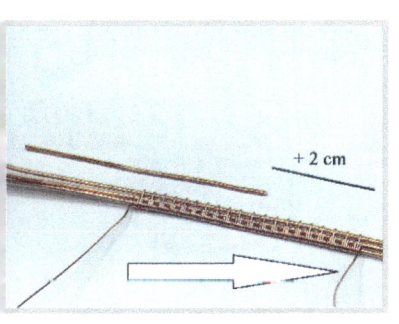

7. Continue to weave, following the same steps, until the woven part is 2 cm longer than the half of the short wire. The center of all wires is aligned.

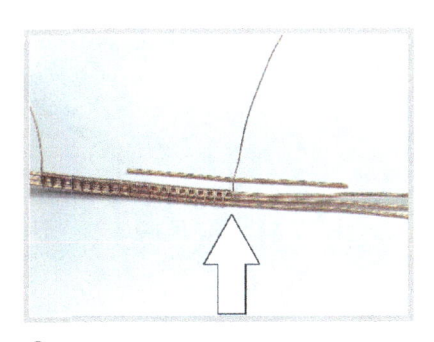

8. Turn the wires from the right side to the left side, clockwise, so the recently made woven part is positioned on the left side now.

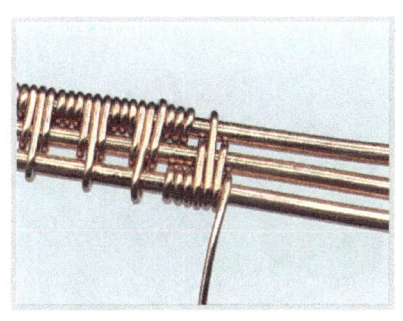

9. With this other weaving wire end repeat the same weaving steps, following the Sun weave technique, as shown here.

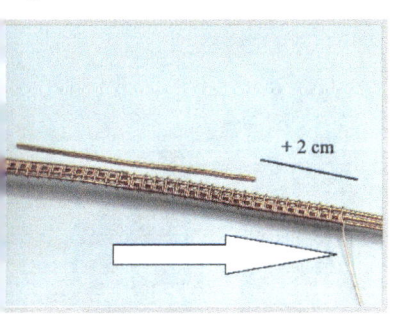

10. With this other weaving wire end repeat the same weaving steps until the whole woven part is 2 cm longer than the half short wire. The whole woven part must be 4 cm longer than this wire.

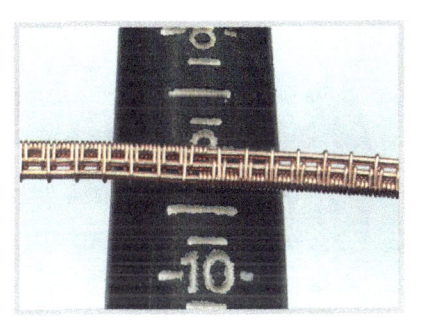

11. Position the center of the woven part over the ring mandrel (or wooden dowel), as shown.

12. Bend both ends of the woven wires all around the mandrel. On the other side, the wires coming from the left must be pointed upwards, the right wires must be pointed downwards.

101

TUTORIALS

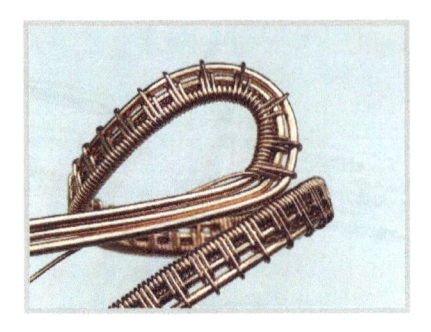

13. Leave a 1,5 cm distance between the upper and lower group of wires. Bend the upper wires into a 1 cm tall half loop, exactly in the same way as shown here.

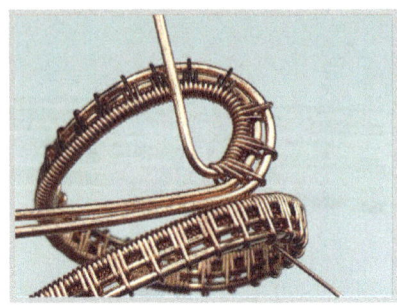

14. Take the upper wire end of the recently bent base wires, bend it completely upwards.

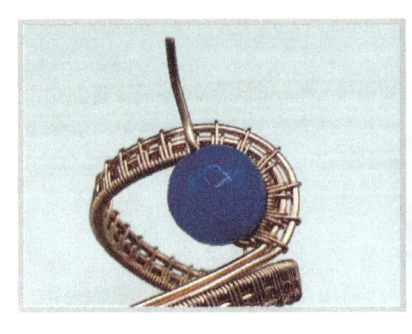

15. Add your bead to this base wire pointed upwards. Position the bead close to the bent woven wires, as shown here. Leave a 1 cm long end on this base wire, cut off the extra wire.

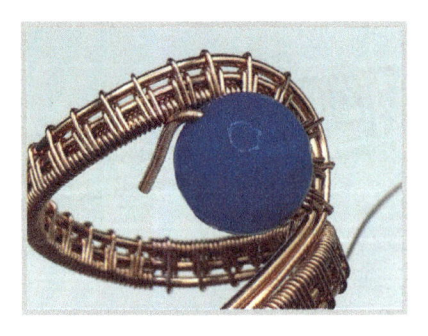

16. With the tip of the chain nose pliers, near the hole of the bead, bend this short base wire end completely backwards, below the woven part.

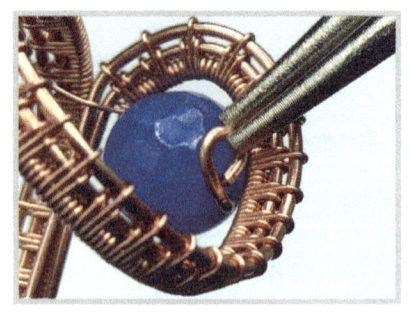

17. Switch to the back view. With the tip of the round nose pliers make a small loop with the base wire end, positioning this loop over the bead.

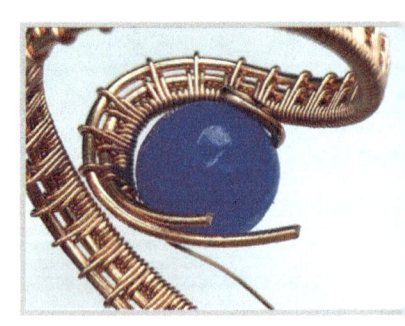

18. Bend these other 2 base wires from the same group below the bead. Leave a 0.5 cm end on the upper wire, a slightly longer end on the lower wire.

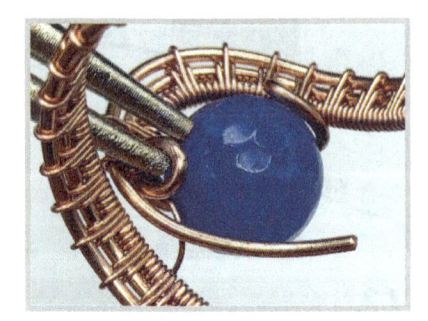

19. With the tip of the round nose pliers, bend the upper wire end into a small loop, positioning this loop close to the bead.

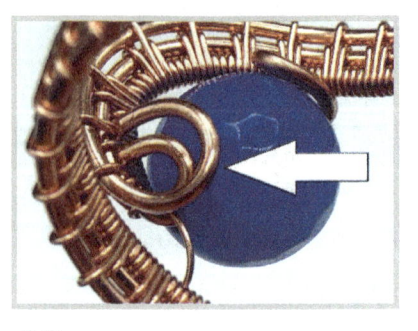

20. Bend this other wire into a loop, bending it around the smaller loop we made before, until it is completely closed, as shown here.

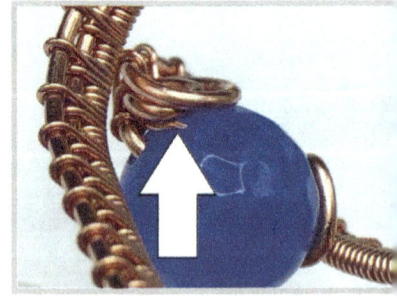

21. Below the bent base wires, cut off the extra weaving wire end on this side. Push the short weaving wire end below the wires to hide it completely

TUTORIALS

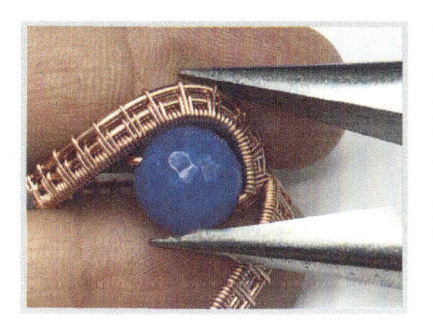

22. *On the front, if necessary, push the bent woven base wires closer to the bead, to avoid any free space between the wires and the bead.*

23. *Bend the other woven base wires all around the lower side of the bead, as shown here. We must make a half loop with the end of the woven part, as we did on the other side before.*

24. *Leave a 0.5 cm long end on the lower base wire, and a slightly longer end on the next 2 base wires, as shown here.*

25. *Separate the bent woven part from the bead, so the wire ends can be positioned below the other wires at the top of the bead, as shown here.*

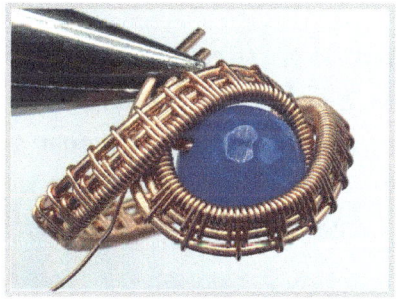

26. *With the help of the chain nose pliers, pull the wire ends slowly upwards, until the bent woven part is positioned close to the lower side of the bead.*

27. *On the back, make a small loop with the shorter base wire end, positioning it close to the other small loop we made with the other base wire before.*

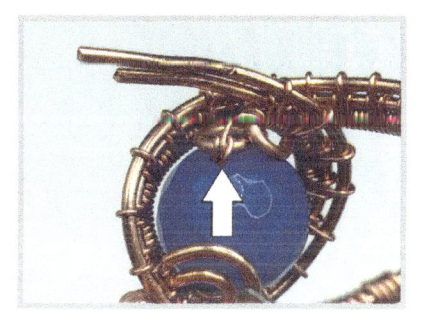

28. *Wrap the weaving wire 3 times around the other small loop, to connect the 2 sides of the woven base wires. Cut off the extra weaving wire end.*

29. *With the help of the round nose pliers, bend these other 2 base wires downwards over the woven part, until they are completely closed. If necessary, cut off any extra wire end.*

Your beautiful ring is ready.

103

Tip:

Always try to stay in natural light when you are crating wire wrapped jewelry. Wire weaving can be eye consuming in poor indoor light and our eyes can get tired very fast. We can sit close to the windows to get a good lightning, so we can save our vision for longer time.

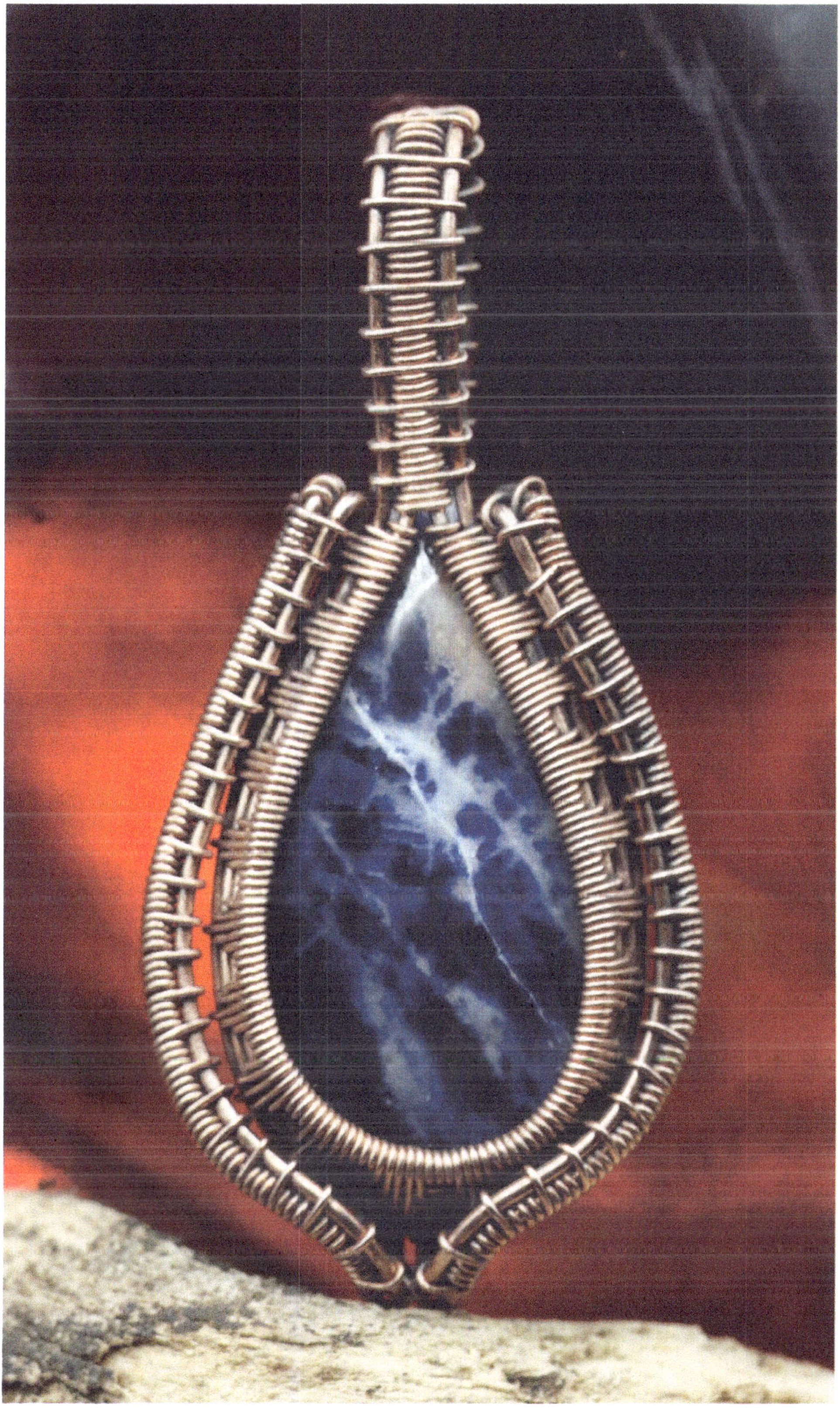

TUTORIALS

Royal Beauty Pendant

In this tutorial you will learn how to create a more elaborated woven stone setting, with the combination of weaving techniques you learned before. For this pendant you will need a a 30 mm tall teardrop shaped cabochon
Tools needed: chain (or flat) nose pliers, round nose pliers, wire flush cutter
Wires: -20ga (0.8 mm) wire: 4x 10 inches (25 cm)
      -26ga (0.4 mm) wire: 1x 100 inches (250 cm), 1x 32 inches (80 cm)

1. Materials and tools for this project are shown on this picture.

2. Cut 4 base wires of the 20ga (0.8 mm) wire, with the length of 10 inches (25 cm), each.

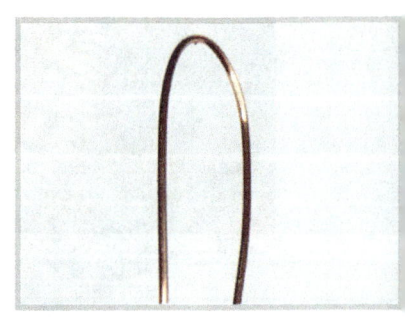

3. Cut a 100 inches (250 cm) long weaving wire of the 26ga (0.4 mm) wire. Bend it in half, as shown here.

TUTORIALS

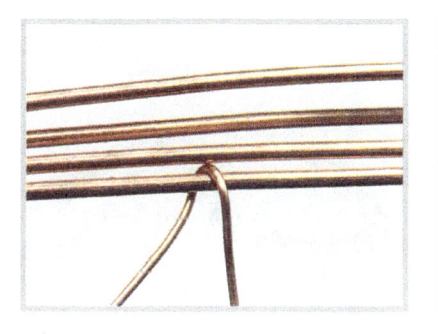

4. Hold the 4 base wires together, making sure that the ends of them are aligned. Position the bent center of the weaving wire around the center of the lower base wire.

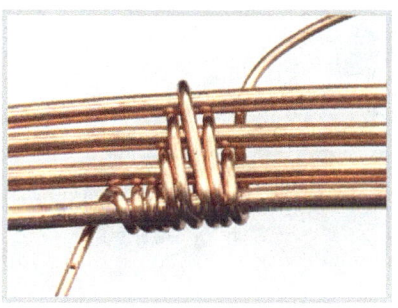

5. With the right end of the weaving wire, make 1 rotation of the Sun weave. Try to weave as tight as you can.

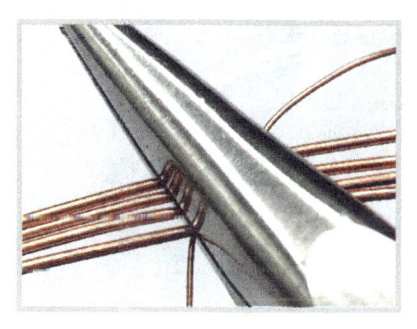

6. Press the woven part with the chain nose pliers, to make it flat.

7. Now compress the weave by pushing it slowly to the left side direction, with the help of the chain nose pliers.

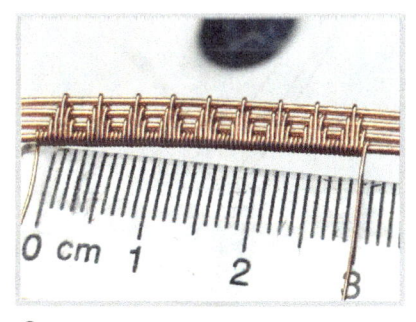

8. Repeat the same weaving, flattening, and compressing steps until you have a 3 cm long woven part on the right side of the base wires.

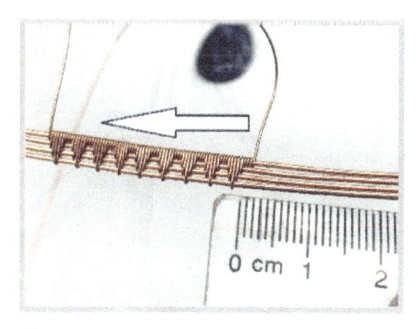

9. Turn the wire structure from the right side to the left side, so the recently made woven part is on the left side from the center of the base wires.

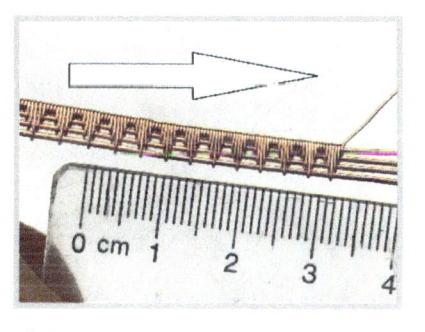

10. Take this other weaving wire end on the right side (which was on the left side before). Repeat the same weaving steps until you have a 3 cm long woven part on this side as well.

11. Position the center of the woven part over the bottom center of the cabochon, as shown. The woven base wires must stay over the stone circumference.

12. Very slowly, we must bend the 2 sides of the woven base wires upwards, bending them around the stone circumference.

107

TUTORIALS

13. Bend the woven base wires close to the sides of the stone, as shown. The woven wires must be positioned over the stone circumference, as they will hold the stone.

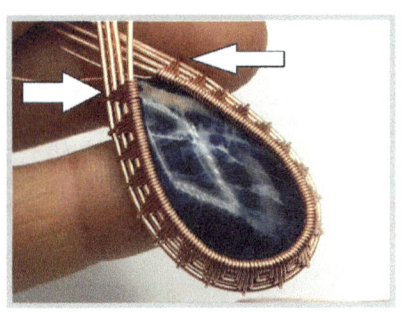

14. If the woven part does not reach to the top of the stone, make another rotation of the Sun weave on both sides. Here I made another rotation until the woven part arrived at the top of the stone.

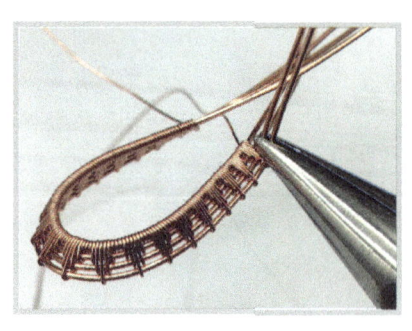

15. Separate the wires from the stone. On the right side, hold the 2 outer wires tight within the tip of the chain nose pliers, bend them forward, as shown.

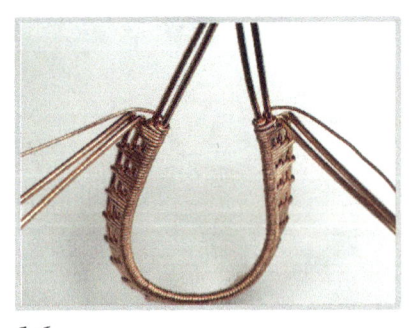

16. On the left side, hold the 2 outer wires tight within the tip of the chain nose pliers, bend them forward, as shown here from the top view.

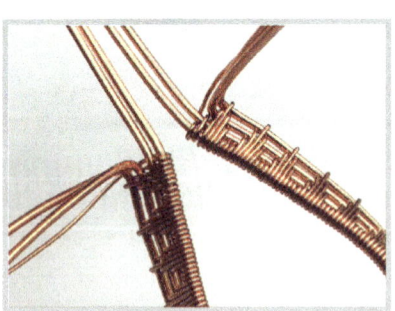

17. On both sides, bend the 2 inner wires completely upwards, then move the 2 ends of the woven parts close to each other.

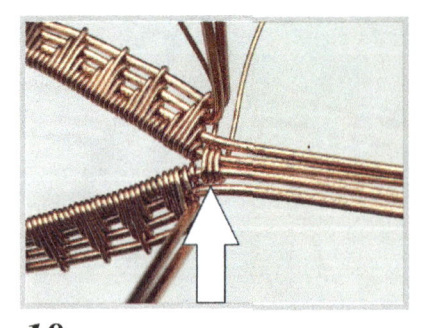

18. Position the wire structure in horizontal. Cut 32 inches (80 cm) long 26ga (0.4 mm) wire. Wrap the initial end of it 3 times around the 2 inner wires of these 4 horizontal wires.

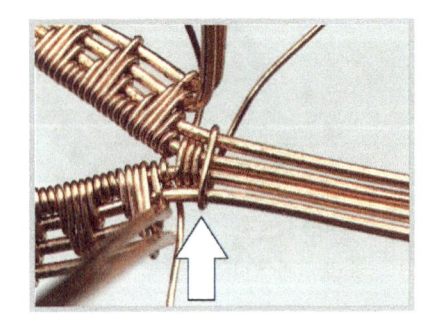

19. Now wrap it once around all 4 wires. This is another variation of the 3-1 central weave, as we learned before.

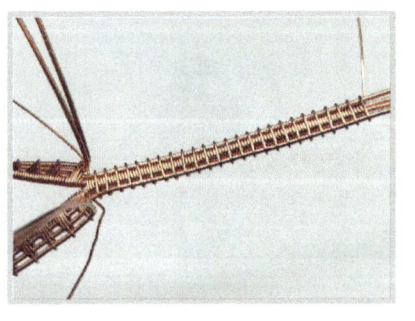

20. Repeat the same 3-1 central weaving steps until you have 25 rotations of this weave, as shown.

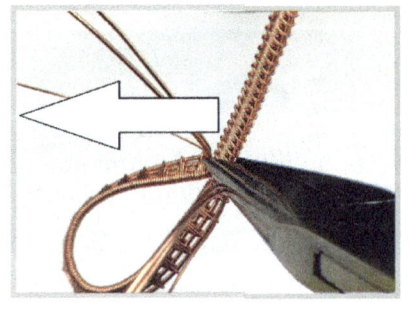

21. With the tip of the chain nose pliers, hold the bottom of the 3-1 woven part tight, bend the woven wires slightly to the front, as shown here from the right-side view.

108

TUTORIALS

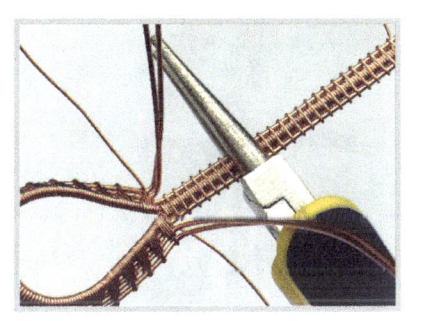

22. At the 8th rotation of the 3-1 weave, hold the wires tight within the bottom of the round nose pliers.

23. Bend the upper side of the woven base wires completely backwards, then downwards, to make the bail of the pendant.

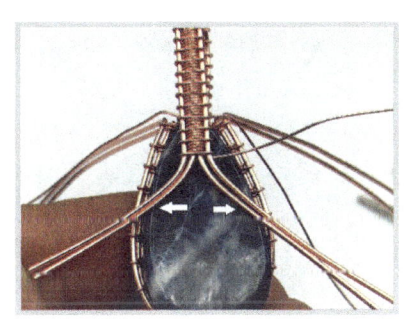

24. Switch to the back view. Insert the stone inside the wire structure, then separate these 4 wires of the weave, bending them to the sides.

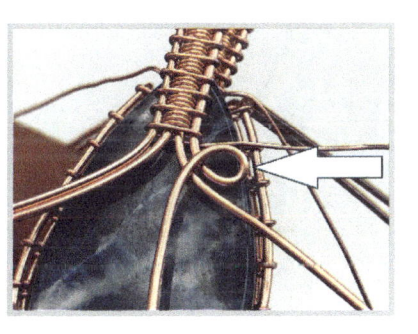

25. On the right side, make a small loop with the upper wire, as shown with the arrow.

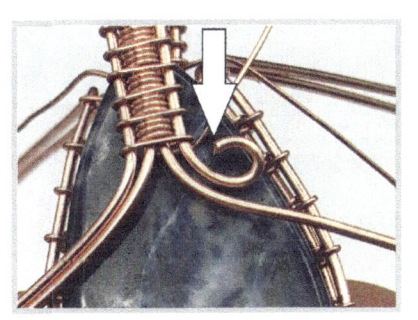

26. On the inner part of this loop, cut off the extra wire end.

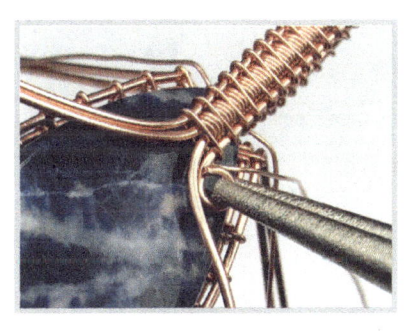

27. With the tip of the round nose pliers, push the wire end inwards, to close this loop completely, as shown.

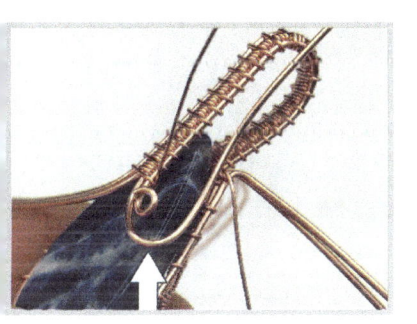

28. Take the other wire on the right side, bend it upwards near the side of the stone, as shown with the arrow. This wire will hold the upper side of the stone.

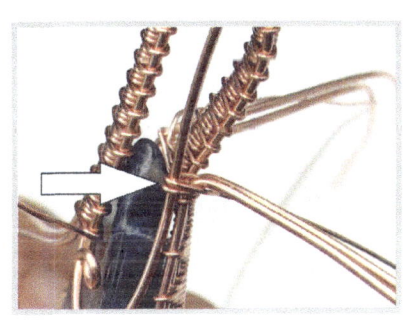

29. Make 2 wraps with the weaving wire around the recently bent base wire and the other 2 base wires pointed to the front, to connect them.

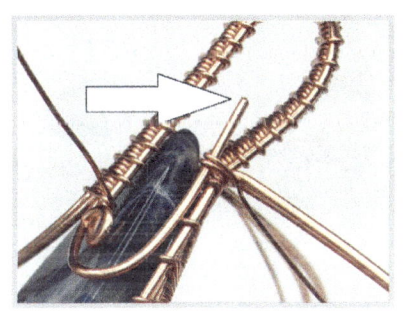

30. Leave a 0.7 cm long end on this base wire. Cut off the extra end of it.

109

TUTORIALS

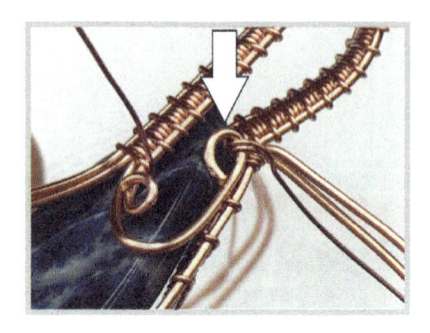

31. *With the tip of the round nose pliers, bend the short wire end downwards, making a closed loop with it, as shown.*

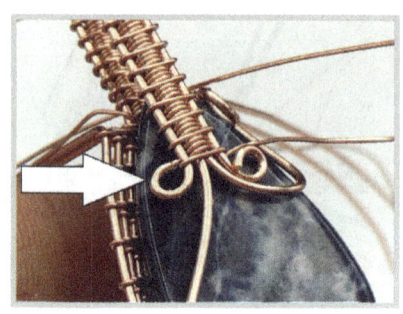

32. *Now we must repeat all these steps on the left side as well. Make a small loop with the upper wire, cut off the extra wire end, then bend the wire end inwards until the loop is closed.*

33. *Bend the other wire upwards near the side of the stone, then make 2 wraps around this wire and the 2 wires pointed to the front.*

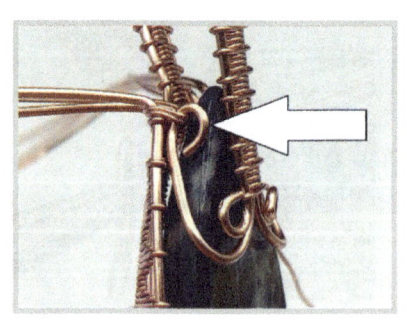

34. *Leave a 0.7 cm long wire end, cut off the extra end of it, then bend it downwards with the tip of the round nose pliers, to make a closed loop with it.*

35. *Separate the stone from the wire structure. On the back, behind the woven base wires, cut off the extra weaving wire end.*

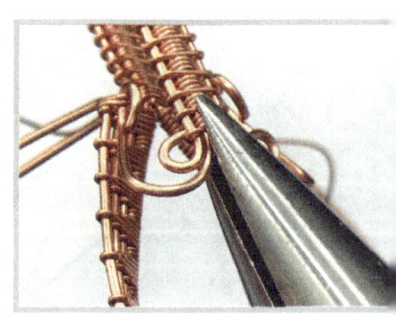

36. *Press the weaving wire end with the tip of the chain nose pliers until it is completely closed.*

37. *From the top view, on the left side of the pendant, we must take the weaving wire and make a 5 cm long woven part of the 3-1 weave, as shown.*

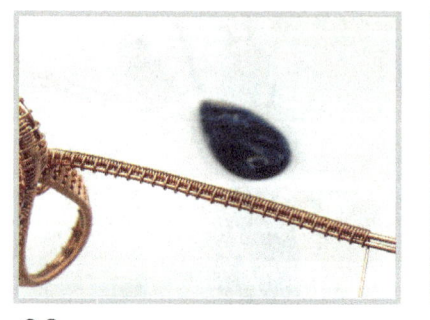

38. *With the weaving wire on the right side repeat the same 5 cm long 3-1 weaving steps, in the opposite way (3 wraps around the upper base wire, 1 wrap around both base wires).*

39. *Insert the stone in the wire structure (optional), then bend the recently woven base wires downwards, exactly in the same way as shown.*

110

TUTORIALS

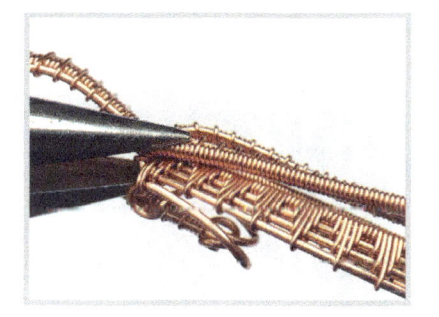

40. Optional step: On both sides press the top of the 3-1 weave to position it closer to the sun weave.

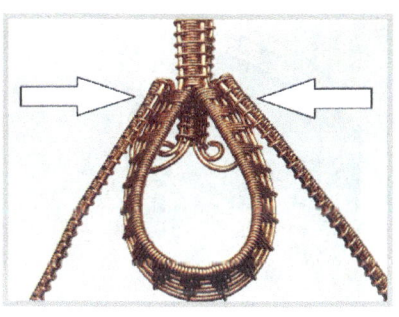

41. From the front view, move the woven base wires outwards, so the top of the woven parts remain on the sides of the 3-1 weave.

42. On the right side, bend the woven base wires exactly in the same way as shown here, making a curve with them close to the right side of the Sun weave.

43. Hold both weaves within the chain nose pliers, so they stay firm. Bend the 3-1 weave backwards at the bottom center of the wire structure, making a curve with it.

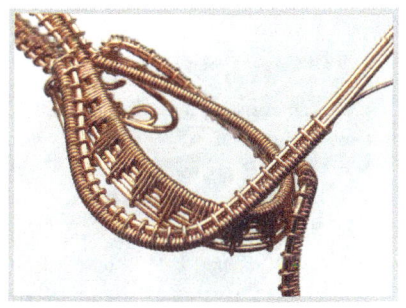

44. We must repeat the same bending steps on the left side as well, as shown here and on the next picture.

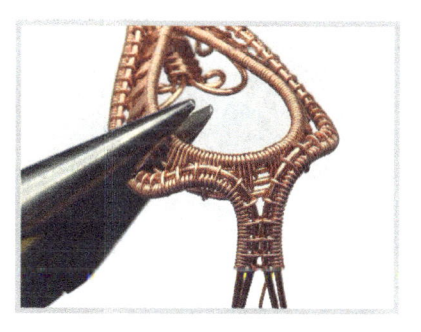

45. The woven base wires from the two sides must be positioned close to each other below the bottom center of the wire structure.

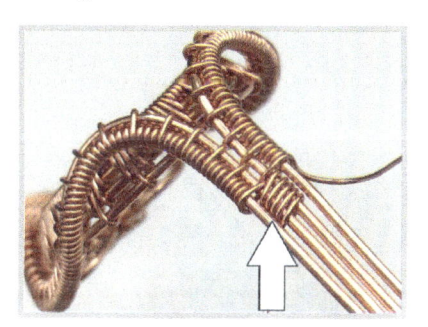

46. With the left weaving wire end, make 5 tight wraps around the 2 inner base wires, to connect the 2 weaves.

47. Switch to the back view and insert the stone in the wire structure. On the front, hold the woven wires tight with your fingers, then push the wire end upwards over the back of the stone.

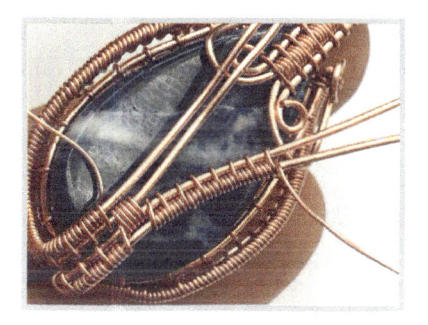

48. With the right weaving wire make 8 rotations around the 2 right base wires, then bend the woven part slightly outwards, as shown here.

111

TUTORIALS

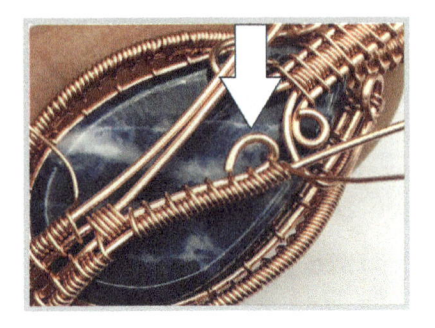

49. Leave a 0.5 cm long end on the inner base wire, cut off the extra end of it. With the tip of the round nose pliers, bend the wire end downwards, to make a small, closed loop with it.

50. Bend the outer base wire downwards over the center of the stone, making a curve with it under the wires coming from the top of the wire structure.

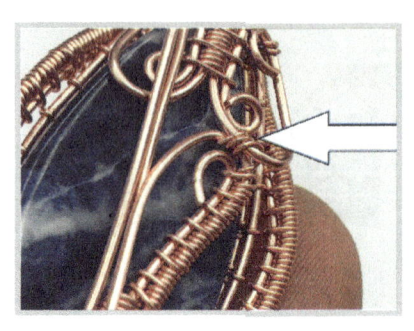

51. On this side, wrap the weaving wire 3 times around the recently bent wire and the top wires, to connect them. Cut off the extra weaving wire end, then press it with the chain nose pliers, to close it.

52. Leave a 0.8 cm long wire end, cut off the extra end of it. With the tip of the chain nose pliers, bend the wire end close to the other wire, to close this loop too.

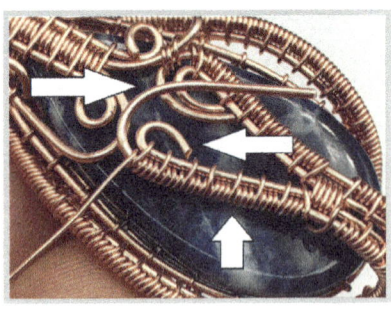

53. Repeat the same weaving steps on the left side as well. Leave a short end on the inner wire, cut off the extra wire end, then bend it downwards, to make a loop with it.

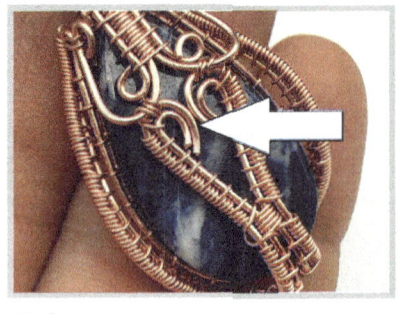

54. Repeat the same weaving and bending steps, to connect this other wire with the top wires and the finish the weaving wire and the base wire ends.

55. On the front, press the 2 woven parts at the bottom center of the stone, to move them closer.

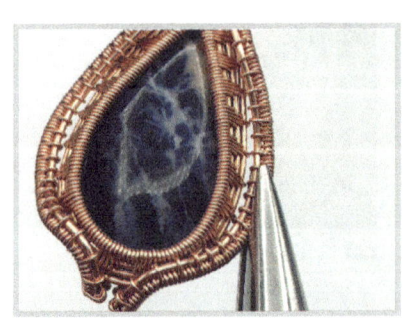

56. If necessary, turn the woven wires to the front with the help of the chain nose pliers, so the weave is more visible.

Your beautiful pendant is ready. Use a leather cord or a chain made by yourself to wear this gorgeous pendant.

112

Getting Inspiration

Wire wrapping can offer unlimited possibilities to create artistic jewelry for any occasion. There are endless options to set a gemstone, how we bend the wires around a stone or bead, what kind of weaving techniques we decide to incorporate in our piece. This art can offer us an immense place to let our creativity flourish. Continuously, we would like to share with you some inspiration wire wrapping pieces, to show you what can be achieved with this art by continuing to learn these techniques. For more inspiration we recommend you visit our website: www.WireWrapTutorial.com , or find us on Etsy: www.WireArtTutorials.com .

About The Author

Erika Pal is the jewelry making projects designer of WireArtTutorials and WireWrapTutorial websites. What began as a hobby in 2016, is now a top jewelry making lessons platform, known all around the world, with thousands of artists joining to learn how to create unique wire wrapped jewelry designs. The shop on Etsy called WireArtTutorials has become one of the best-selling online shops, offering lessons and DIY kits from beginner to advanced levels.

Erika is a self-taught artist who began to experience wire wrap art in 2016 while she was traveling around Europe with her family. She began to create decorations and wire masks, but her interest was quickly complemented by the creation of jewelry of all kinds. She likes all styles, from art deco to classic, from the simplest to the most extravagant. Her most favorite creations are the wire wrapped animal jewelry, like the elephant, owl, dragon, seahorse, dolphin, turtle and many more.

She lives off-grid with her family, in the middle of a forest, getting artistic inspiration from nature. Erika hopes to write her next book soon, teaching more elaborated techniques within multiple intermediate and advanced tutorials.

Made in the USA
Coppell, TX
27 February 2024